Sacred Girl:

Spiritual Life Skills for Conscious Young Women

by

Kenya E. Aissa, MS

Sacred Girl: Spiritual Life Skills for Conscious Young Women

Cover design by Angela Lofton Moore – InfoPrincess

Cover art & Illustrations by Amelia Souva

Editing by Katie Quarles – Get it Edit

Published in the United States of America

Sunshine Solutions Publishing
9912 Business Park Dr., Ste. 170
Sacramento, CA 95827

Library of Congress Control Number   2018949148

ISBN-13: 978-1721786145
ISBN-10: 1721786147

Acknowledgments

It's been a long journey to get this book written and into your hands, so the list of people to thank is really lengthy, and no one has that kind of time. I'll summarize it instead, and you're welcome. First, to my publisher Phillis Clements, and my editor Katie Quarles, you two are an amazing dream team for which I'm very grateful. My friend and incredibly talented illustrator Amelia Souva, you and your art are such a blessing to me and to everyone who sees your work.

Most importantly, I have to thank my OGs, my original girls, my fun, silly, crazy caseload: Sonya, Leigh, Leticia, Demetria, Heather, Meghan, and Navdeep. There were many others who came through the doors of Daytop Village, now Our Common Ground, and whom I was blessed to work with, but you were my main babies. I love every one of you to the moon and back, and fortunately, you all still know this, all these years later. This is for you, and all the girls who came after you.

Also, thanks, and much love, to Dr. LaNae Jaimez, who hired me as the counselor for Daytop's Women's Program. I don't know what you were thinking when you hired me, and I had no idea what I was doing. Fortunately, this didn't deter you since clearly you saw something in me. Thanks for encouraging (i.e., tolerating) my unconventional way of doing things (most of the time) and being a compassionate, uplifting presence to the kids and to me. Thanks to my incredible friends!!!! I really love all of y'all. Holly Warren-Mordecai—girl, I love you so much it's not even funny.

Who else would actually book a hotel room with a bay view so her friend could smash writer's block and write the last 11 pages of a book? I truly have no words.

To Laura Loomis and Stephanie Carr, my writers' group, your support and feedback were invaluable. Thanks for being on this journey from the beginning! Thanks to my parents, Carollyn Gay and David Bradford, for always trying to guide me in the right direction, and still supporting me when I totally ignored you and did whatever I wanted to do. I know you think I'm both awesome and weird, but you have only yourselves to blame. Big thanks to all of my godchildren, especially Jasper Alexander Guzman, who helped me both with the book and with the many mysteries of the Internet.

Thank you to Our Common Ground in Redwood City, for providing a safe and loving environment for so many youth on their recovery journey over the decades. Huge thanks to my best friend, ride-or-die, forever-Bestie Erica Guzman, for having my back in every way possible for 25 years. I love you more than I love tacos.

Last, but definitely not least, thanks to my amazing husband Bob Aissa for his unwavering support through the many jobs, incarnations, and totally out-there ideas of his wife. You are the best husband, father, and partner in the world.

Introduction

Why are you reading this book? Something led you to the place that you are now, where you are either a) curious about spirituality; b) the victim of some busybody do-gooder who thought this book might be good for you; c) the recipient of a nice gift; or d) a sucker for a pretty book cover. Whatever your reasons may be, you are here now. WELCOME! Glad you could make it to the beginning.

What's this book about, anyway?

Let me begin by saying that this book is for all girls—adolescents, teens, and young women—who feel as though they are spiritually disconnected. Specifically, this book aims to address girls who may have been knocked off of their spiritual path through traumatic experiences, dysfunctional families, or unhealthy relationships, as well as girls who have no idea what a spiritual path is. This book was initially inspired by the amazingly strong and beautiful young women, who I still refer to as "my girls" or "my caseload," that I worked with when I was a counselor at a residential rehab facility in California. Ladies, you know who you are! Some of them gave me lots of grief, some of them just went along with the program, and others made me want to rip my hair out. But all of them taught me something about women, and about myself. Since that time, I've been able to pay their gifts forward, many times over. The lessons that my girls taught me have found their way to many young women. It is a very deep well that holds my gratitude. A great woman, poet, and teacher, and one of my "she-ros," Maya Angelou, said, "A person who is not use*ful* is use*less*. You must be of use to someone other than yourself." My spiritual path led me to my girls, my students and teachers that followed them, and to writing this book. My sincere hope is that I can be useful by helping girls and young women enrich their lives by honoring their spirits, and finding their own paths.

When I began facilitating a spirituality group for teen girls who exhibited symptoms of Post-Traumatic Stress Disorder (PTSD), I was surprised at the confusion that arose when we first put the word "spirituality" on the table. Is "spirituality" just a fancy word for religion? Does it mean engaging in some sort of hocus-pocus? Does it mean sitting around and meditating on the stars, chanting "Om...om..."? Does it mean airy references to "my inner self," or "my aura"? Do I have to be able to read tarot cards or run with wolves?

You may be pleased (or not) to find out that the meaning of spirituality is up to *you*—in other words, what it really means is whatever makes YOUR spirit *breathe* or come alive. So now you know that the responsibility, and the power, is in your own brilliantly capable hands. This idea that we hold so much responsibility for our own paths can be a scary one. So much so that there are those who barely lift a finger to propel their lives in the direction that they want to go. Some people genuinely feel that everything is in the hands of their higher power, fate, or the universe. So why bother trying? Let me share the Sacred Girl school of thought: the universe needs a hint. Your higher power could use your input. No matter what you've been told in the past, or what story you've been living out in the present, you are never powerless. It takes only action to show you just how powerful you really are. If you toss a pebble into a still pond, the ripples that your action creates are too many to count, and the effect is surprisingly far-reaching. Think of yourself as the pebble—small, when you consider the grand scheme of things, but strong for your size. Think of the pond as your life—the endless possibilities, and your ability to hold others up while still getting to where you're going. Your life can go in many different directions, and it's up to you what you prioritize, what you decide to accomplish now, what you decide to save for later, what you ditch in favor of a new idea. I'm not suggesting that success, abundance, or fulfillment is easy. But it depends on what your definitions of those words are.

The word "spirit" comes from the Latin word *spirare*, which means, "to breathe." Spirit is not referring to your body, or your physical self, but your *life principle*, or your soul. Just as each of us has our own soul, each of us has our own unique and individual way of making our souls come alive. When our spirits are breathing, we are better able to connect with our selves, other people, and the world around us. So, maybe for one person, spirituality does include chanting, or lighting candles, or reading the tarot, or just looking at the stars. Who am I to judge? I can do only what is right for me. However, unless you are a circus performer or work in a wildlife preserve, I suggest you leave running with wolves to…other wolves!

For many women, the process of feeding the soul traditionally comes by way of organized religions, of which there are thousands from all over the world. There are thousands, possibly many thousands, of religions just in the United States. And the offshoots! Just as Sikhism is a Hindu religious sect, Catholicism is a form of Christianity. Imagine what the rest of the world holds in the form of religious beliefs. Many "non-traditional" religions are also widely prevalent, such as Wicca (Witchcraft), Voodoo, and Hare Krishna, and belief systems commonly referred to as cults. I will very briefly discuss some of these religions in this book in the form of a quick overview, purely for the sake of providing information for the curious. However, this book is not about religion, so I will not dwell on it.

This is not a deeply intellectual or clinical book. It is written with you girls and young women in mind, for you to be able to understand it and relate to it, so you can decide for yourself what works for you. There may be things written in this book that people in your life don't approve of. To those folks, I can say only that this book is in no way meant to disregard or undermine the system of beliefs in your family. On the contrary, it is meant to encourage an open mind for the reader, and an open dialogue between the reader and others. This is for *you,* the girl whose spirit is suffocating. For whatever reason, you are spiritually disconnected. You may have been hurt, abused, or gravely damaged. You may have been raped. You may feel as though friends, family, or God has deserted you. Your self-esteem may be at an all-time low. You may have grown up watching too much reality television, and it skewed your perspective and values. The purpose of this book is to show you that if you are connected to your spirit, you can be connected to your God or Higher Power, your family, friends, culture, and the earth, in a way that gives you peace and joy that can't be matched by money, sex, drugs, gangs, beauty, popularity, or the "perfect" body. So, on that note, I just have one thing to say: *Breathe, Spirit*! *Breathe*!

1.
CHAPTER ONE:

What's the Point?
Your Spiritual Journey

"Being on a spiritual path does not prevent you from facing times of darkness. But it teaches you how to use the darkness as a tool to grow."—Unknown

You may be asking yourself: "What's the point of exploring spirituality?" This is a good question. And the answer is, there are many different reasons to explore spirituality. When you explore your spirit, you explore your *self*—you discover what's important to you, what your passions are, what kinds of things make you feel good, and what makes you feel sad, empty, and lonely. You may be thinking, "I already know these things about myself!" But embarking upon a spiritual path requires more than seeing the obvious, which is what's so exciting—and so scary. It is a journey, and it takes a serious commitment. When you fall off of your path, do you give up, or worse, beat up on yourself for flagging periodically? NO! I mean, do we really want to look that deeply into ourselves? The answer is a resounding YES! I'll use myself as an example: one thing that I love to do is go to secluded beaches, especially if there are large rocks to sit on that overlook the water. Now, I could stop there, and just say, "I love the beach." Or, I could do a little self-exploration. Why do I love being alone on the beach? What's happening inside of me when I look out to the horizon, when I listen to the seagulls squawking, and when I hear the waves crash against the shores? I especially love when there are tide pools so that I can look for hermit crabs, starfish, and sea anemones. Why do I get such great satisfaction at touching these small creatures and watching them go about their business? I've found through the years that being around water makes my spirit breathe; it makes me feel alive, and helps me to see that I am part of the earth, just one of its many beings, but significant in my own small way. Maybe every trip to the beach doesn't give me such intense insight, but it makes me feel good just the same. The smell, the breeze, the sounds, and the rare opportunity to just sit and listen to the earth do its thing—I love it! There is power in silence, and clarity in solitude. That's why meditation is such a big deal. What better way to get to know yourself than hanging out with yourself, listening to your own thoughts, feeling your feelings without a lot of distractions? But we'll talk more about meditation later.

Besides reaping the many benefits of self-exploration, there are other reasons to find your path. When you are learning about yourself on a deeper level, it's like you are in school for the rest of your life, but the only subject is you—welcome to "ME 101"! Class begins immediately, and never ends. This is how you begin to structure your life. The people you allow into your life, the people you become close to, the energy that enters your room or your home, even how you decorate: these things can either feed your soul, enriching it with positive energy, or sap the juice right out of you. The good news is, it is completely in your power what you allow into your spiritual environment.

It is true that we all have "soul suckers," a.k.a. "spiritual vampires," in our lives. They can be relatives that we see once a year, roommates, acquaintances, and sometimes, unfortunately, our own immediate family. It is the people closest to us who affect us the most, and sometimes the effect is very painful. For those of us who have been, or are being, abused or neglected it is especially hard. Often, girls feel that there is no escape from the harsh reality of their lives. Others may use spirituality as a way to escape their real lives. I hope this book will help you to find a balance between rebellion (which can be dangerous, even life-threatening) and withdrawal (which can be a sign of depression, and just as dangerous). There is a healthy middle ground, and it's called "Peace."

Women of all ages give away their power to other people by taking in harsh criticisms, constantly trying to please others by acting a certain way, or struggling to reach the unattainable goal of looking "perfect" in order to be applauded by society. How ridiculous is this? While you can never control what another person says about you, you can control how you allow it to affect you. Just as you would not allow a legion of roaches to take over your kitchen, you should never allow "toxic people" to stomp their dirty boots on your spirit. It is up to you to decide if you want the people in your life to be positive, affirming, and loving people (notice how I keep putting the responsibility on *you*).

Take a look at the qualities in people that you are attracted to. Below, circle words that describe people that you want to be around:

positive	exploring	culturally rich
creative	simple	romantic
athletic	peaceful	religious
musical	grounded	fun
environmentally responsible		intellectual
humorous	adventurous	political
traveling	artistic	affectionate
outgoing		

Add any necessary words that I did not include—it is *your* list, after all. Put a check next to the words that describe characteristics that you would like to cultivate for yourself. Next, put a star next to words that describe you, as you see yourself right now.

SIDEBAR

It is imperative to acknowledge your own positive qualities. Many women tend to downplay their strengths, either out of fear of appearing boastful or immodest, or out of fear of offending someone else. We should ask ourselves, Why are some people so threatened by the power and vibrancy of certain women? How often does society stifle young men or boys? Not as often, and that is fortunate for them. This is what I call "oppression through suppression," and I, for one, have had enough of this garbage. We, as women, are encouraged by society to buy into this way of thinking, and we are even rewarded for it. Don't believe the hype! Stand up for yourself and proudly acknowledge the gifts that God, Goddess, or your

Higher Power has so generously bestowed upon you. I am not saying that women should brag about themselves all the time, because that's just obnoxious. Humility is an important part of maturity. However, so are honesty and pride.

The purpose of the above exercise is to help you focus on what type of human energy you want in your life, and it's easier to focus on what we want when we name those things. If you were not raised in an environment that was nurturing and safe, there may exist within you a spiritual emptiness. It is now essential to your journey that you create, and welcome, energy in your life that is spiritually supportive. In part, that means blocking toxic energy, and welcoming positive, loving energy from others.

Identifying Toxic Energy

One foolproof way to discover if the energy around you is toxic is to examine your feelings honestly; if you find that certain people or situations make you feel like crap, then you are probably surrounded by toxic energy. If you frequently feel unworthy, low, or depressed, then something has to change, and the sooner the better. We all find ourselves in life situations that are necessary and unavoidable. There will always be times when someone is unkind to you, or a work or school environment becomes overwhelming. Welcome to life, honey! The good news is, these things are *outside* of your inner self. Work and school are not life, but they are a necessary part of life, and they are tools to help you earn a living and reach your goals. Rarely do we have any other choice but to face things in our lives head-on, so we may as well make the best of the frustrating aspects of life. You are not able to control what others say or do, or the negativity that others put out into the universe. Having an active spiritual life will enable you to better manage the outside world by helping you to cultivate an inner peace.

Think of your spirituality as being a soft, protective bubble around you, filled with peace, love, and glowing warmth. Your bubble morphs itself to allow positive, healthy energy to enter, but is completely impermeable to the negative stuff that tries to get in. Your bubble is strong, and refuses to break. When all else fails, you know that your bubble is there, and nothing can take it away from you. Even if you choose to step outside of your bubble for a while, it rolls around behind you,

16

invisible, but there, just in case the need arises for it to wrap you up again in protective love.

Meditation, Journaling, and Affirmations

There are many tools available to help you block toxic energy. The three that I will discuss here are *Meditation, Journaling,* and *Affirmations*.

"Meditation" literally means "deep, continued thought, or deep reflection on sacred matters as a devotional act" (Webster's *New World Dictionary*). You probably already meditate, even if you are not aware of it! When I first realized how important solitude at the beach was to me, I had no idea that I was meditating. Contrary to popular belief, meditation is not something that is strictly practiced in Eastern religions. When I was eleven years old, my Catholic schoolteacher (a nun, no less) taught my class about meditation, and I started doing it at home. It can be very relaxing, and it can help center you when are feeling disconnected or frazzled.

If you have never tried to meditate, start with a simple exercise. Sit somewhere that is comfortable, safe, and free of distractions. You may want to sit in front of your altar if you have one, or on your bed with your back against a wall. Lighting candles helps to set a relaxed mood, as does soothing music. My personal choice of music to meditate by is a CD that plays beach sounds, with a classical music background. Not surprisingly, the sound of seagulls and pounding waves is perfect for me, and I use the same CD almost every time I meditate. I suggest using music without lyrics, because you might accidentally begin to sing along, taking the focus away from your own inner dialogue, and shifting it to the words in the song.

When you are comfortable, close your eyes. Breathe deeply, feeling your chest expand and contract as you inhale and exhale. Think of a word or phrase that you want to meditate upon: *Love, God heals, Arms of the Mother*, or anything that helps to ground you in spirit. You can breathe *in* thinking the first part of your phrase, and breathe *out* thinking the second part of your phrase, or any rhythm that feels natural to you. Allow yourself to just sit, and feel the weight of your body on the floor or bed. Continue to breathe, and listen to your breath sounds.

When you are involved in a **self-centered** exercise (that phrase is not always negative) such as meditation, you are learning to block toxic energy by creating positive energy through a self-loving activity. *You strengthen your spirit every time you take time out just for yourself.* When your spirit is strong, it is difficult for harmful vibes to reach you. It's like when you rub sun block all over your body to protect your skin from sun damage—you can use a sun block with SPF 15, or go for the heavy-duty armor, SPF 45. You know those harmful ultraviolet rays will have one heck of a time getting through the SPF 45! But you have to keep reapplying it for it to be effective. Similarly, you have to keep strengthening your spirit by giving it your time and attention, as often as possible.

Another way to meditate is to focus on your body as you breathe. This can be a very uncomfortable exercise for many girls, especially if you feel like your body is your enemy, or if you have been physically violated in some way. If you choose this exercise, and it brings up scary emotions for you, I urge you to discuss the feelings with someone you trust, such as a close friend or counselor. Writing down your feelings immediately after the exercise may also help you to understand your reaction.

You can begin by breathing deeply, as in the previous exercise. Breathe in through your nose, and out through your mouth. Concentrate on your toes, and then feel the energy work its way through your feet to your legs. Focus your energy on your thighs, then move to your groin area, up through your belly, to your heart. Concentrate on the rhythm that your heart makes as it beats. Move the focus of your energy to your breasts, around to your back, and up your neck. Feel the energy in your cheeks, lips, nose, eyelids, and forehead, all the way to the top of your head. Imagine that you can feel each strand of hair, and that each strand is alive with energy. Continue to breathe as you feel the weight of your body. This is a good exercise to "own," or reclaim, your body. You can think about each body part in turn, claiming each part as you work towards your head. When your energy focus has reached your head, you can continue to breathe, now feeling your entire body relax as gravity pulls you to the earth. Recall which, if any, part of the meditation was uncomfortable. How did you feel as you claimed each body part as your own?

Examining your feelings after meditating is one way to begin Journaling. Researchers have been studying the benefits of journaling for over 20 years. Journaling entails honest, open writing about your deepest feelings. It's pretty much the same thing as keeping a diary. For spiritual purposes, the focus of your writing can be on your *inner* life. As I stated above, you can write about how you feel during meditation. Do any painful issues come up for you? Does it make you feel empowered? Does meditating make you feel calm? Remember that it is *your* journal and *your* feelings. Be honest.

A fun and easy way to use journaling to block toxic energy is to write about any spiritual experiences that you had during the course of a regular day. This helps you to keep your eyes open to the beauty and life essence of the world around you. Instead of just plodding ahead on your way to school, look around. What kinds of flowers are growing in your neighborhood? What's the weather like right now? How does the breeze feel on your skin? Take the time to walk outside. If you pass a tree, touch its bark. Is it rough and dry, or soft and mossy? Are there tiny bugs burrowing in and out, or ants marching briskly in line? Think about the roots of the tree, and how deeply they are planted in the earth. Every day, interesting, beautiful things happen all around you. These occurrences can be ordinary, like the sun shining overhead, or extraordinary, like a colorful rainbow. Are you noticing them happen? If not, why not? These are things to write about, and questions to ask yourself, in your journal. These are only examples, though. Your world is full of spiritual energy coming from many different sources.

FIND THEM! Only you can identify what makes your spirit breathe, so when you come across it, acknowledge it; don't ignore it.

SIDEBAR

I don't know about your household, but there were some serious privacy issues in my home that eventually made it impossible for me to be sure my journals were confidential. I have learned through my work with teen girls that the fear of someone else reading a journal can actually stop the writer from writing altogether. There is a solution to this problem, but it takes some creativity. One of my favorite tricks is to write very private things in a language that the other members of your home do not know. I know it's sneaky, but who wants that nosy little brother reading your innermost musings? And think of how impressed your parents and teachers will be if you suddenly reveal an interest in Latvian! Another solution is to create your own secret language, which is what I did. Sometimes I combined Spanish with Pig Latin, sometimes I wrote backwards in French. The upside to all this hard work is a) I was assured that my thoughts remained my own, and b) to this day, I excel at learning new languages!

It will be easy to begin writing if you have a journal that represents you. There are literally thousands of different journals to choose from. Some are floral, some have natural fiber or hand-made paper, and others have fun designs or humorous sayings in them. You can usually find journals at your local bookstore. Often, neighborhood bookstores or specialty gift shops carry journals made with unique designs and materials.

Rarely have I found a more useful tool for blocking toxic energy than Affirmations. The core purpose of this book is to encourage the reader to empower herself by finding her own spiritual path, even if she is in emotional pain, or a negative environment. Affirmations are verbal acknowledgements of people, things, or ideas. When you affirm yourself, you might say to your reflection in the mirror, "I will hold my head up high today." Commonly referred to as "positive affirmations," you can say a word or phrase to yourself with the specific intention to make yourself feel good: "I am beautiful and strong, and I am proud of myself." There are times when all of us struggle with a particular burden, and you can recite an affirmation to deal with that burden: "With faith, strength, and self-love, I will survive my ordeals." Even a phrase as simple as "I can make it!" can be useful. Affirmations remind us who is in charge of our minds, bodies, and attitudes: ourselves. I'm sure you know that if something is repeated to you often enough, you start to believe it, right? When the soul suckers of the world say, "you're stupid," or "you're worthless," or make us feel that way by abusing or violating us, it makes us feel so low that we believe their lies.

Affirmations are a way for you to channel spirit through positive words. The best thing about affirmations is you can do them anywhere, at any time. It's almost like praying. Through prayer, we communicate with our Higher Power, Earth, or The Spirit to give thanks, or to ask for help with things that we feel are beyond our control. With affirmations, you are reaching into yourself for strength. As an exercise, begin every day for a week with an affirmation. It can be about the beauty of the world, your own inner strength, or whatever you choose. Record your affirmations in your journal, and write about the effect, if any, the affirmation had on your day.

If you need a little help, never fear. The internet and books are great sources of affirmations for everyone, from people of certain cultures, to people with addictions, to victims of crime. So give it a try! You have nothing to lose, and much to gain.

2.
CHAPTER TWO:

Begin at the Beginning

"In creating, the only hard thing is to begin: a grass blade's no easier to make than an oak."—James Russell Lowell

Of course, there is more than one way to begin your journey. The answer to the question, "How do I start?" is this—JUST START, ALREADY! Meditate, breathe, smell, move, sing, sit and be still, or whatever feels right to you. Remember, once you have begun, the wait is over. Spirit is waiting for you, even if you have been resistant, or disinterested, or had a bad attitude, and you can seek it out whenever you are ready.

When you examine your life today, where do you feel you are in your spiritual journey? Are you at the beginning of your journey, and ready to find your path? Are you still in the questioning stage ("Do I really want to do this? Am I ready to be committed to having a spiritual life? Does this take a lot of work? Will spirituality make me vulnerable, soft, or open to getting hurt?")? Have you felt like you have been following a certain path, but that it no longer works for you, or wasn't really your idea to begin with? Maybe you were raised in a family with strong religious beliefs, rituals, and traditions that are comfortable for you, but you are somehow not feeling it the way you would like to. It is one thing to believe in God, or a Higher Power; it is another thing for your beliefs to give you a sense of peace, safety, assurance, and love. Let's face it: most of us were raised to believe what our parents believe, and we carry on with those general beliefs and traditions without ever questioning them. When we aren't questioning something, it may mean that we aren't giving it much thought. And where your spiritual beliefs are concerned, you don't want to be lazy.

Shanti's Altar

Shanti was a 14-year-old with a troubled past. She had a hard time trusting me, her counselor, and an even harder time sharing her story honestly with her peers. She openly participated in her spirituality group, largely because it involved writing, which she enjoyed, and lots of self-expression through drawing and other creative activities. One thing that I found fascinating about this young girl is that she was in a constant state of creative motion—if she wasn't writing a poem or a story, she was drawing. She also loved to dance, and would often borrow one of my long scarves to twirl around herself while she moved to music. Creative activity made her feel safe. When she was unable to find an outlet for her creative energy, she became anxious, and high anxiety was an ingredient in her recipe for disaster. She would cut or scratch herself, or engage in other self-destructive behaviors. I worked with her on developing relaxation techniques to lessen her anxiety. As she explored different forms of spiritual expression, she discovered that she felt most connected to Witchcraft, also known as Wicca. Wiccan traditions are earth-centered, and very grounded in respect for Mother Earth and all of her creatures. Shanti was also somewhat attracted to the non-traditional, spooky reputation of Wicca, and the fact that it seemed as "different" as she felt. When she and I began to discuss her desire to become more spiritually grounded, she came up with a brilliant idea: to utilize her unique, artistic style for an important element in the spiritual path: creating the *sacred space*, or *altar*.

What exactly is an altar? An altar is an area where a person has assembled objects that are meaningful to that person. In a spiritual context, these can be ritual objects; religious symbols; artifacts; photographs; things collected from nature such as feathers, seashells, rocks, or pinecones; memorabilia; or things that lend to a certain aura that you want to create, such as candles, incense, or water. You are creating a physical vehicle by which to transport yourself to a spiritual state of being. So that the journey will have a purely positive beginning, keep your altar free of "negative" energy and objects: no *stolen* items, no matter how pretty they are! No items that remind you of past *bad behavior*! Steer clear of items that remind you of an *embarrassing or shameful* time of your life, and nothing that brings up *extremely painful* memories. Your altar is to help you connect to Spirit, not to pain; you should utilize the services of a trusted therapist or counselor to help you do that. This is not to imply that items you choose to adorn your altar should not make you feel anything. For example, a photograph of a lost loved one may bring up pangs of loss, but also an underlying sense of love that brings you more joy than pain. Your chosen items should help you move forward along your path, not drag you down.

Almost any surface can be used as an altar. One woman may use a windowsill, while another may use an old desk, or the top of a dresser. You can also utilize the space around your altar, like the walls—hang a picture above it or install a little shelf for a scented candle. My altar is a cute, old bookshelf that I bought at a flea market when I was in my early twenties. It was a hideous, dirty-yellow color, but it has an unusual shape that attracted me to it. I bought paint remover and scrubbed until the beautiful natural wood came through. Although I had never refinished anything, I went to the local tool-lending library and checked out an electric sander. I missed quite a few hard to reach spots, but after I painted clear varnish over the whole thing, I was very pleased with the fruits of my labor. It has looked the same since, and I am currently planning to paint it a pretty, robin's egg blue. I have assembled many things that I think are beautiful, and reflect my spiritual as well as worldly beliefs. These include tons of seashells and rocks from various beaches; marbles; a red jade Buddha (a gift from one of my sacred girls); another Buddha made from a very rare jade that my mother picked up for me on a trip to China; a porcelain Quan Yin (the Chinese goddess of compassion); a crucifix and two rosaries that belonged to my husband's grandmother; and a large, broken Italian tile with a huge stone Virgin Mary on top. Part of the fun is that it is a work in progress, and, like me, it changes, evolves, and becomes more interesting with time.

It is widely believed that *personal altars*, as opposed to the grand, multi-statued, glittery gold displays at churches, temples, and other houses of worship, are women's territory. Families of various cultures have long, rich traditions around the altars passed down by their foremothers. Because the altar is a physical representation of what you feel is sacred, the resulting connection to the Divine is intensely personal. This is important to keep in mind as you decide what you want to put on your altar, and even what you want it made out of. Every part of your altar is significant.

The Buddha said, "Faith is the beginning of all good things." I had a gut feeling that Shanti's altar would be interesting and full of color and texture, so I encouraged her to have faith in herself and her choices. She decided to create an altar in her bedroom. Shanti was delighted by this process, and it was definitely a process. As time passed, she added new things, or removed things that she felt were no longer appropriate for her. She rearranged things, changed the scent, color and shape of the candles, et cetera. On her altar, which was really a chest-high dresser, she assembled various items special and meaningful to her. These included a vibrant silk fabric covering, a pentagram, dried flowers, candles, pictures of her little brother and sister, a tiny skeleton of a baby bird, a tarot card that I gave her, and some shells and feathers from a trip to the beach with her class. She truly felt grounded in her own unique connection to the Spirit when she lit the candles, prayed, or performed rituals.

All of us are creative beings, especially you. Think about it: you, as a girl, are the most complex and exciting creation of nature. What else can walk, talk, sing, give birth, and nurture? Okay, maybe a parrot, but you get my point. So, if you have not yet tapped into your creative gifts, and you are beginning on your path, setting up your own personal altar is a good start. If you take a look around your bedroom, you probably already have things that are altar-friendly lying around. Even something as simple as a rock can be the first item on your altar, if it holds special meaning for you. If you don't already have something that feels sacred or special to you, make something. This is definitely one way to honor the creative goddess in you! Draw a picture, write a small list of spiritual goals on a pretty piece of paper and decorate it, write a poem, or jot down the lyrics to a song you love. If these ideas don't appeal to you, or you get stuck, take some time out and ask yourself what you are feeling. If you feel silly or embarrassed writing down personal things, start very small and work your way up. For example, write one spiritual goal and fold it up. This sacred space is just for you, so take all the time you need. It is your space to feel grounded, to feel the presence of the spirit, and to allow yourself room to contemplate and connect. Do not rush your creative goddess; she is always with you, and will magically appear when you need her.

Identifying Your Goals

A spiritual goal is like no other. When we use the word "goal," it's usually meant to describe something that, when reached, the effort is over, like finishing high school, getting into the college of your choice, or landing your dream job. "At last, I am HERE!" you may cry out triumphantly, fist in the air. The peace, fulfillment, and connectedness that come from following your path will hold much greater meaning for you than worldly successes. Although I admit, my dream job of being a professional chocolate taster would fulfill me to no end, I would not trade my countless spiritual rewards for training day at the Hershey factory. In other words, instant gratification is not always the answer. There is a saying that goes, "It's not the destination, but the journey." You may, in fact, have many goals as you travel along your path. In order to identify them, ask yourself:

Is my life missing something?

Do I usually feel at peace with my life?

How do I feel about myself?

Am I important?

Do I feel a general sense of safety in the world?

Is my environment supportive?

Do I come from a religious family?

What are my family's spiritual practices?

How do I feel about my family's spiritual practices?

Do I believe in a Higher Power? Why or why not?

Just as an example, say that one of your goals is *Inner Peace*. Don't laugh! I know it sounds generic, but let's face it—there are few things as satisfying as that. What I mean when I say "inner peace" is true self-acceptance, the ability to soothe yourself when you are hurting, and the capacity for genuine forgiveness. One of the most important lessons you'll ever learn is this: *you can only change **yourself***.

So, if you put yourself down, hate your body, or call yourself stupid, you are working against your desire for inner peace. When you are hurting and you stew in the anger for a long, long, LONG time, you are choosing to work against inner peace. Don't fret—many people do this! Everyone gets angry, everyone gets hurt, and everyone hates it. Frankly, I don't even think it's natural to immediately take a deep breath, calm yourself down, and think peaceful thoughts when you feel bad. Furthermore, a healthy dose of anger can cause you to make positive changes in the way you accept treatment from others.

However, if you sit in sadness, self-pity, and negative thoughts, you will soon notice that your suffering is not going anywhere! You will be in inner turmoil, not inner peace. If you practice talking about how you feel to people you trust, and engage in activities that help your spirit breathe, you will have more peace in your life. For some, this may be an unimaginable goal. Getting to know your true self through self-reflection, open and honest inner dialogue, and maybe a little journaling thrown in for good measure, can help you on your way. Always remember, your goals are just steps along your *journey*. I hope that you continue this journey for the rest of your life! Why? Because there is so much to learn, and you are always evolving and growing as a person. Only you can decide how you will proceed.

Some people believe that if you struggle to stay on your spiritual path, or if you fall off, you have failed. You have now become a spiritual statistic! But the old adage "If at first you don't succeed, try, try again" can be put to the test at these times. These little slips, like most little slips, are learning experiences. If you wander from your chosen path, take some time to reevaluate your situation. What are the circumstances that made it challenging to stay focused? How can you avoid wandering from your path the next time these circumstances present themselves? Because believe me, the challenges will keep on coming. The tragedy doesn't lie in the slip-up, any more than success lies in an unwillingness to accept mistakes. Don't try to be perfect! Loving yourself is an important part of this journey. Positive affirmations, forgiveness, self-acceptance, and pampering are important parts of loving. Get it? Treat yourself with as much care as you would the most important person in your life, because that is exactly who you are.

Play the FANTASY LIFE GAME!

As a child, my favorite board game was "LIFE." The players get to choose great jobs, have as many children as they want, and do fun and exciting things as they traveled in the little car throughout their "lives." To this day, I love to fantasize, daydream, and make up exciting, romantic stories about myself and other people. I didn't realize it when I was younger, but I was actually practicing a type of *visualization*—I was beginning to identify, by playing a game, what I wanted in life. Obviously, it's much harder to get an education, secure an interesting career, and raise kids than it is to move from square to square on a piece of cardboard. But focusing on reality while playing a board game would have been no fun, and would drastically defeat the purpose! Letting your fantasies go to extremes can be fun. Try it:

Get out your journal, or just a piece of paper and a pen. Get comfortable in a place where you can avoid distractions. This level of fantasizing takes focus! Remember, this is your own fantasy life scenario, not a life that you'd want for your mom or your best friend. It's admirable if you yearn to work for world peace, but save the deep and meaningful stuff for later on. Now, answer the following questions:

What is my fantasy job?
Would I be single in my fantasy life? If not, who would be my fantasy sweetheart?
What does my house look like? Do I live in my current town? Hollywood? Bora Bora? Paris?
What kind of car do I drive? Or, what does my chauffeur drive? Do I get everywhere on foot because I live on a cute, tiny island where I don't need a car?
Do I have any kids? Pets?
What are my favorite hobbies or activities?
What foods do I eat? Do I harvest and cook my own food like Martha Stewart, or do I have a personal chef like Oprah?

Okay, you get the idea. With these questions in mind, write a day in the fantasy life of yourself, from the time you wake up until you go to bed. It doesn't matter if your day is spent fishing, dancing, or hanging out with friends; it's all about you. It can be as descriptive as you want, or just a few sentences, but try to hit all of the highlights as you see them.

Yes, this exercise has a hidden agenda. Its purpose is to use the grand gift of your imagination to visualize extraordinary possibilities. I realize that it may be somewhat of a stretch to imagine that you will live in a 25-room mansion with a full staff, doing little more than eating bonbons all day in front of a flat-screen television.

As life teaches us, money is definitely not the key to happiness. But what this may say about you is that you desire financial success. If your fantasy is to leave city life behind and survive off of freshly-caught fish and herbs, maybe that says that you enjoy simple, peaceful living without the pollution and stressors of the daily grind.

Read your story, and identify the parts of the scenario that you feel are possible with a little persistence, hard work, and luck. Not *probable*, but *possible*. It's too easy to shrug your shoulders and say, "That probably can't happen." I saw a dancer on television who had lost one of her legs from the knee down, and she continued to dance professionally using a prosthetic leg. She was so talented, graceful, and confident; it was like nothing was missing! But she had overcome seemingly insurmountable odds to make her dreams come true: a devastating illness, the loss of her leg, and everyone telling her that it was ridiculous to

35

pursue a career as a dancer without an intact body. Well she showed them, didn't she? Even if you don't have a burning desire to make a particular dream into a reality, you must realize that the *possibilities* are endless.

Write down the steps that you would have to take to reach one of your fantasy goals. Do the steps include some sort of training? Or maybe just a lot of practice at a certain skill? The steps you take must be yours to take; you shouldn't say, for example, "I can reach my goal of owning a music store if my grandfather gives me $10,000." While this may be true, that's a lot of responsibility to put on old Gramps. Maybe you need to get a job in a music store, learn a little about business, or talk to people in the know.

If you find that the more you write down the steps, the more your goal seems less like a fantasy and more like a possibility, then I guess I have reached *my* goal—helping you to visualize a life not without pitfalls, but without limits.

3.
Chapter Three:
The Body

"I think that what is happening to me is so wonderful and not only what can be seen on my body, but all that is taking place inside."—Anne Frank, *The Diary of Anne Frank*

The Trouble with Chapter Three

I have a confession to make.

Subconsciously (I think), I have avoided this chapter like the plague. I knew that I wanted to speak to young women and girls about our bodies, and how we are so affected by our own body images that we can actually harm ourselves in pursuit of a "better" body. I wanted to discuss anorexia, bulimia, stress, sex, self-hatred, plastic surgery, and self-care. Oddly, I found myself writing *around* these issues, instead of facing them head-on. It was illuminating to find that despite my passion regarding women and self-esteem, despite my disdain for society's death grip on controlling how we see ourselves through current fashions and trends, that I, an educated adult, can still be reticent, even afraid, to confront these issues. How very, very sad. How disappointing to discover that age, education, awareness, and spiritual connectedness are not necessarily enough to render a woman immune from the disease of fear and discomfort about body image. It's actually painful to discuss. It hurts me to watch one of my best friends repeatedly brutalized by anorexia. It hurts me just as much to watch another young friend jeopardize her health by eating her way into morbid obesity because she doesn't feel important enough to prioritize her health. My own bulimia left me with the unique ability to throw up without even sticking my finger down my throat. I am tired and dispirited that for girls, negative body image is a monkey on our backs that won't be shaken off. Let's talk about it anyway.

First, the facts. We all know that puberty and adolescence are challenging for both boys and girls. But there are significant and disturbing differences in the ways we respond to the physical changes:

* Girls are less happy with their bodies and have more negative body images than boys throughout puberty.

* As puberty continues, girls' dissatisfaction *increases* due to increase in fat, while boys' dissatisfaction *decreases* due to an increase in muscle mass.

* By age 15, girls have *twice* the rate of depression as boys.

* The few studies that have focused on female hormones indicate that increased levels of estrogen are linked to depression in adolescent girls. Unfortunately, it's not all about hormones. One study shows that *social* factors contribute to girls' depression and anger 2 to 4 times as much as *hormonal* factors!

Those are the statistics, the facts as they exist in this world outside of ourselves. What can we do to rise above our pains, before they destroy the power that is our feminine birthright? We can reclaim ourselves by allowing the love of our Higher Power to enter us. We can channel this love through prayer and self-care. Our bodies, the sacred vessels that we were temporarily gifted, are easily damaged from a lack of love and appreciation. Besides all the "too fat/too skinny" stuff, our bodies can be harmed just from the effects of negative emotions, especially when the negativity is directed inward.

You know that feeling when you are anxious, and you get a knot in your stomach? That is an actual biological event where chemicals are released in your body and your brain. Just ask anyone with ulcers about the effects of stress. I had an experience years ago that really showed me up-close how important it is to give more love to my body. I had a devastating breakup with my boyfriend, and one day I realized that my hair was falling out. Now, it took a while for me to notice, since at the time I had enough hair for five people. But one day, I was brushing my hair and noticed a tiny bald spot at the top of my head. I didn't immediately make the connection between my heartbreak and my hair, and thought that maybe I had singed off a chunk with my extra-hot curling iron. It had been known to happen before, so I wasn't alarmed. As time passed, though, the small spot got bigger and bigger, until it was about an inch wide, and smooth as an egg. I even had to do a little "comb-over," clipping the long hair on one side over the spot with a bobby pin.

I finally went to my hair stylist, Janice, who said I had a condition called Alopecia. She said in my case, it was probably my body's way of telling me to pull myself out of my pain and take care of myself, mentally and spiritually. She said, "It's one thing to be single; you can live with that. It's another thing to be single and *bald*." I agreed with her wholeheartedly. She said, "I don't care what you have to do—take long bubble baths, light some candles, whatever—but start taking care of yourself."

It's funny that my stylist could do double-duty as a wise sage, and encourage me to do rituals! I found that the bubble baths and candle-lighting promoted quiet reflection and prayer, and there grew an alliance between my spiritual self and my body. If I cared for my spirit, and took the time to breathe and listen to my own inner dialogue, then my body followed the path of peace and serenity created by my spirit. My hair came back slowly and crookedly, and I learned a valuable lesson along the way: it's important to travel this life with a full understanding that your spirit is the real you, and your body is the finite flesh-and-bones container for your infinite spirit. Regardless, we don't want our containers to fall apart any sooner than nature, good luck, and sound judgment intend them to.

Extreme Fakeovers

I don't know how it happened, but it seems like overnight we turned into a plastic-surgery-obsessed society. And not just in the U.S.—China has a Miss Plastic Surgery Beauty Pageant! Not too long ago, cosmetic surgery was primarily for cancer survivors, accident victims, and celebrities. Now, you can finance a boob job and get liposuction on your lunch break. The trend that has me completely flummoxed, though, is cosmetic surgery for teens, even children. My friend had her first nose job when she was only ten. I was shocked when she showed me a picture of herself before going under the knife. I expected to see a nose that was so huge or misshapen as to be likened to a birth defect, or at least something that kids would tease her mercilessly for. Instead, I saw an adorable little girl with a perfect face. I could shake my head only in distress at a culture that would pass down three generations of unnecessary surgery to a ten-year-old cutie pie.

I'm not going to take the time to lament where we went wrong, the media's part in this quest for sameness (because it is truly not a quest for perfection), or why someone would risk their life for tight abs. I don't care about where we went wrong, but I do care about the future of you girls, and encouraging you to be your own definition of beauty. Taking back your uniqueness; owning your physical beauty because you can honestly identify things that you love about your face and body; and doing your best to live a healthy and balanced lifestyle is real empowerment. If you have a physical characteristic that is devastating to you, or getting in the way of your leading a normal life, then I believe that medical intervention is a very reasonable option. But cosmetic surgery is still surgery, and therefore carries a lot of risks. The trend of teens getting cosmetic surgery is one that I would like to see reversed. Remember, as young women, you are still growing and changing. Growing up is naturally awkward for many people, but part of growing up is discovering your personal style and creating the image, or images, that you feel express who you are. When you are hyper-focused on your physical appearance at too early of an age and pick yourself apart to see what you can change, you are taking away energy that could be spent on creativity, spirituality, and dreaming grand dreams. Everyone wants to be attractive, but do we all have to look the same?

SIDEBAR

Do a Body Affirmation where you look at, and touch, your entire body from head to toe. Tell each part what you like about it, what you appreciate about it, and how you are going to love it every day. What did your legs do for you today? Did they work hard to get you up a hill, as mine did? Think about stretching out your hard-working quadriceps as a tribute to their hard work. You can thank your body simply by grooming yourself and having good personal hygiene. It's fun to make a ritual out of Body Affirmations, including lighting candles around your bathtub before you get in, to ease the day's tensions.

Eating Disorders

By the time most girls reach high school, they know a little bit about eating disorders. The most well-known are **Anorexia Nervosa** and **Bulimia Nervosa**, usually referred to as simply "anorexia" and "bulimia." However, obesity can also result from having an eating disorder.

Anorexia involves the relentless pursuit of thinness through starvation. Some of the danger signs of anorexia are:

* Having a major fear of gaining weight that does not go away with weight loss.

* Weighing less than 85% of the average weight for a person's age and height.

* Having a distorted body image, or thinking that your body, or parts of your body, are fat when they really aren't.

Usually, girls that are anorexic have a tendency to be competitive and high-achieving. They get stressed out when they struggle to reach their own high standards, and worry about what other people think of them. Since weight is something that can, for the most part, be controlled, many girls turn to weight loss to feel more in control of their lives. Unfortunately, they lose control, until their quest for more weight loss becomes an illness. The sicker an anorexic gets, the more difficult it becomes to regain healthy eating patterns. Very recent studies show that in many cases, anorexia is also due to genetic factors. This is in sharp contrast to the traditional school of thought that anorexia is solely due to psychological issues. In extreme cases of anorexia, a girl can lose her hair, lose bone density, stop having her period, grow fine hair all over her body (a reaction that the body undergoes in order to keep itself warm), and start having heart palpitations and chest pain. Most girls (about 70%) recover from anorexia, but the road to recovery can be years-long and require multiple hospital stays and lots of psychotherapy. Many girls, even after they recognize that they have a problem and try to change, are still unable to recover. At this stage, a girl can die from a heart attack or some other type of organ failure.

Bulimia differs from anorexia in that a person with this disorder is not as restrictive with their food intake. Instead of starving herself, a bulimic girl will often eat regular amounts of food, or even binge on huge amounts, and then "get rid of it" by throwing up or using laxatives. This cycle is called *bingeing and purging*. Because the girl is not starving herself, this disorder is often hard to detect. Most bulimics stay within a "normal" weight range, so people close to them are not usually alarmed by a rapid weight loss. Just like with anorexia, about 70% of girls or women who suffer from it will recover. Bulimia can also lead to major health problems and even death. The stomach acids, from frequent vomiting, can eat away at the lining of your esophagus. Acid can also destroy the enamel of your teeth. I saw a woman on television with an extreme case of bulimia: she had lost all of her teeth, was completely bald, and was unable to have children.

A national survey conducted in 2010 concluded that 34% of adolescents in the U.S. are overweight or obese. Studies show that both heredity and environment contribute to obesity. It's easy to understand how Americans can get so out of shape, what with food deliveries, the internet, and other energy-saving products and services that don't require us to move. Economic factors (poverty and level of parental education being significant) are also relevant. But just like anorexia and bulimia, obesity can be the result of stress, depression, and anxiety. The health risks involved with obesity are numerous: heart problems, joint problems, colon cancer, and Type 2 diabetes, just to name a few. Several studies further suggest that higher rates of obesity may contribute to lower attainment of education and higher poverty rates. Although this is not mentioned in these studies, I feel it's worth stating that obesity has nothing to do with intelligence or IQ levels. Obviously, one can certainly be overweight and highly intelligent. Furthermore, there are many women in the U.S. who are overweight, but very active; consider themselves quite healthy; and are happy with their bodies. No one perspective is absolute. There can be a huge disparity between how a person feels in their body, and how the medical field views them. My point here is that body image, whether you're underweight, overweight, or considered a "healthy" weight, can affect the way you move through, respond to, and interact in this world.

Having an eating disorder is only one way that women and girls take out their stress and anxiety on their bodies. There are many others (drugs, risky sexual behavior, alcohol abuse, etc.), but one way of dealing with emotional problems that is just as solitary and isolating as an eating disorder is *cutting*, or self-mutilation. I have known many cutters, both in my professional life and personally. Not surprisingly, cutters have many of the same characteristics as anorexics and bulimics, namely perfectionism and a desire for control. Many cutters become so stressed out by their personal problems that the only way they can deal with their emotional pain is by masking it with physical pain. For some girls, they feel so disconnected from their physical bodies that they cut themselves just to feel alive. Often, the sight of their own blood reassures them that they are living beings.

Self-destructive behaviors are strongly linked to a lack of spiritual connectedness. Again, spiritual connectedness is VERY different than religious involvement or activity! Let's be real: for some people, their spirituality is deeply connected to religion. For others, there is no connection; in fact, some people are so disconnected from religion that they want no part of it, but they still feel a connection to their Higher Power on a personal level. When stress, the pursuit of perfection, and outside issues are the center of your life, emotional problems are sure to arise. If you are more focused on your internal life, your gifts, self-love, and connection with your Higher Power, you will have less time and inclination to focus on what's "wrong" with you, what needs to be fixed, and what other people are thinking about you.

If your spiritual life is being enhanced through self-awareness, prayer, meditation, and connection with people and activities that feed your soul, you will be less inclined to strive for perceived perfection. You will know that you are already perfect! This knowledge is found in the peace, serenity, and love that you draw to yourself by allowing your spirit to be the center of your life. Now, don't get me wrong—if you are suffering from an eating disorder, or if you are engaging in any type of self-harming behavior, you must seek professional help! Your life and health are much too important to take lightly.

Studies have shown that spiritual connection can contribute to healing both physical disorders and disorders with their roots in emotional dissonance. However, there are medical and mental health professionals who specialize in all aspects of these disorders, and it is always best to consult a specialist to help you determine the best plan of action. Remember: eating disorders can be deadly. It is best not to play around with them, so if you think you may have one, seek help. If you think someone you know may have an eating disorder, or is otherwise hurting themselves, encourage them to get help. If they don't, here is a situation where you take responsibility for your fellow girl—*tell on her*. I couldn't care less how unpopular this may make you, or how pissed off the other person may get. Her life is far more important than her liking you, so get over it, and tell on her to her parents, a school counselor, a physician, or any responsible adult. If you continue to see the behaviors, tell again until you have informed every adult who is in a position to help. It is ultimately the responsibility of the adults in the girl's life to make sure she receives the appropriate help.

Gender Identity and Body Image

Dr. Cary Gabriel Costello wrote in his blog, intersexroadshow.blogspot.com: "Truly unnatural things do not occur, so they generate no outrage squads decrying their transgression." I had to read that several times to gain what I hope was an understanding of what he meant. My simplistic way of seeing issues of gender identity, transpeople, homosexuality, Third Gender (i.e., Two-Spirit, Hijira, etc.), the question "What is your pronoun?" and pretty much everything else about a person's identity is this: There are no mistakes. There is no right or wrong in gender identity or sexual orientation. There is what is, and that's for each individual person to understand for themselves, and explain to others should they need to or choose to. Of course, this is my personal opinion, and everyone is entitled to theirs. It has forever boggled my mind that one can be raised in a religious household, learning and believing that God is all-powerful, that He created everything and everyone, is the purveyor of all things miraculous and awesome, but on these issues, He had an off day. Like, God slipped up and made gay people. Or last Tuesday He had the sniffles, so His game was off and he accidentally stuck a newborn girl in the body of a newborn boy. Oopsies! Or worse, everything that "we" believe is good, is the work of the Lord. Everything that "we" believe is bad, is the work of Satan! In my opinion, this logic is ridiculous and a complete waste of time. Furthermore, if you believe in God and see Him/Her/It as all-knowing and all-powerful, then you can't also see Him/Her/It as capable of having an off day. God doesn't make mistakes, so prejudice against one, or a group, of God's people is silly. God made them, period. Whether anyone likes it or not, young people are grappling with gender identity issues every day. They always have, and they always will. I am not a geneticist, a biologist, or anything remotely close, so I can't explain why gender identity issues exist or where they begin (Sperm? Egg? In-utero? Pre-utero?). Nor do I care to. What I do plan to do is continue to support and love people how they are, and where they are in their journeys. Denying, disparaging, or hating any part of a person's identity does not make the person turn away from the "offending" identity and switch to the identity someone else has assigned to them or thinks they should have. It really doesn't work that way.

For young women who are coming out as transgender (a different gender than they were assigned at birth), as gender non-conforming (presenting and/or behaving in a way that is not clearly male or female and possibly identifying themselves using non-gendered pronouns), or as gender non-binary (an expression of gender that is neither male nor female, or not exclusively male or female), there can be very unique struggles regarding their bodies. There was a time when people assumed that a person "born female" (assigned the gender of female at birth based on the appearance of their genitalia, and usually meaning they were born with a vagina), then later identifying as male or something "not female," would opt for gender reassignment surgery, a.k.a. a sex-change operation. That is not necessarily the case, and often, young women and even girls are choosing to forgo surgery for a variety of personal reasons. Many people feel that the outward appearance of their bodies doesn't have to jibe with their gender identity. All of that being said, there are enormous physical, social, and psychological challenges that come with identifying one's gender as one that is not accepted, or expected, by friends and family. This topic is too important, and too complex, to fully delve into within the confines of this book. Therefore, I strongly recommend that if you are experiencing gender identity issues; concerns; or questions about your own gender identity or sexual orientation, find a SAFE person, professional, therapist, doctor, or organization to help you. Let me be clear that this may take some time. You may go to a person or organization for support and find that they are not supportive of your identity or your effort to live authentically. Move on and keep looking until you find people who support you and will have your back. Your tribe is out there. I've included some resources at the end of this book for you to reference if needed.

Taking It All In: Your Senses

The five senses are *smell, sight, taste, touch,* and *sound*. All of them join together to make your body a fragrant, tasty, loud, hot, cold, hungry, painful, pleasurable, dark, bright place to live. If you want to create spiritual connections, you have to first be connected here on earth to your body, your environment, and the people in it.

Smell—Have you ever smelled something and it made you feel a certain way? Have you experienced "déjà vu," which is the sense that something has happened before? Maybe the smell triggers unpleasant feelings in you. How about a city smell, like exhaust and fast food restaurants, or the scent of a person's cologne? Smells can elicit emotions like happiness, fear, sorrow, and loss. They can even make you feel nauseous, dizzy, aroused, or hungry. The sense of smell is a vital part of your connection to your environment. Smells go straight to your brain, and your sense of smell is the one that you have the least control over.

Sight—Do you see beauty when you look out your window or ugliness? The sense of sight is a phenomenal gift in many ways, and it's one that we don't often take time to really appreciate. Try to remember the last time you looked outside and thought how pretty the blue sky was. Has it been a while? It may seem like a small thing, but when you raise your awareness of your visual surroundings, life takes on a greater meaning. You become more a part of your world when you see what's happening in it. Not that everything around you has to be pleasing to the eye. Sight is not simply about what you see in front of you. It is also about perception— what you perceive when you look at something. Just because I may not find beauty in an object does not mean that it is not beautiful to others. Some of the finest works of art are considered great because of their very abstract qualities. This is the same point that I brought up when we discussed your sacred space: some things that you see as beautiful may be uniquely to your taste. That makes those things all the more special.

Touch—Imagine things that feel good to the touch: a kitten, a baby's skin, your favorite blanket. Maybe the texture of your own hair feels good to you, or the wind caressing your skin. When other people touch you, it is usually a good feeling, like your grandmother hugging and kissing you, or your coach patting you on the back for a job well done. Good touches can make you smile, or sigh with pleasure. In no other way do we connect with our surroundings so intimately. When we are children, we are often taught about "good touching" and "bad touching," good touching being touches that feel comfortable and non-intrusive, and bad touches being those that make us feel uncomfortable or scared. Remember that your body belongs to you and only you. That includes every part of your body and every hair on your head. It is completely unacceptable for someone to touch you in a way that makes you feel bad, or to touch you intimately without your consent. Of course, as we grow older and mature, most girls enjoy kissing and being touched by someone that they have romantic feelings for. But you must be aware of your own physical and emotional boundaries, and make sure that people with whom you are involved know where you draw the line physically and sexually. If anyone does not respect your boundaries, it doesn't matter how sweet they act, how cute they are, or how cool they seem— give them the boot. There is never an excuse for disrespecting you, so don't accept any excuses and don't make exceptions to that rule. If you compromise yourself to make others like you, it will eventually backfire on you. Most people respect those who respect themselves.

Taste—Ahh, the sense of taste, my personal favorite. I love good food more than anything. Besides being used to nourish our bodies, food is used all over the world in rituals, community gatherings, and religious celebrations. Every culture has its food traditions. For example, you probably know the phrase "As American as apple pie." Here in the States, we eat a lot of fruit pies, while in many other countries, people eat pies made with meat, vegetables, eggs, and beans. Fortunately, America is a melting pot, rich in its various cultures; here, we have access to all sorts of food. People connect spiritually over food when they pray to bless their meal, or to thank their Higher Power for putting food on the table. What you put into your body is important to your spiritual, as well as your physical, well-being. When you eat plenty of healthy foods and drink lots of water, you are showing love to yourself via your body. I know that junk food can be a lot of fun, and sadly, Americans are fast-food connoisseurs. Furthermore, we are not always raised to think of food in terms of it being directly linked to our health. There are medicinal herbs and vegetables such as garlic, turmeric, and beets that are good for us; the unfortunate flip side to this is fast food, fried food, and processed foods high in sugar and salt that actually harm us. The short-term hit to our health can show up in our feeling sluggish and bloated, or suffering from migraines or depression. Long-term issues can include unhealthy weight gain, diabetes, and high blood pressure, as well as liver and kidney disorders. Moderation is key, as long as we err on the side of caution by filling up on real food. If we develop our sense of taste to appreciate and love freshness and variety, we will make this sense work for us in a positive way.

Sound— Each of the five senses is an incredible gift. The sense of sound, however, is twofold. You can hear sound and you can create sound. Your voice is a tool, a healer, a weapon, an instrument, and a teacher. Speaking words out loud emits energy into whatever space you are in. What kind of energy do you want to put out into the world? Some people use prayer to channel energy through their voices, thus creating powerful changes in themselves and their spaces. In Judaism, cantors use their voices in a melodious, musical tone to pray during religious services. Using your voice, you can ask for guidance, strength, world peace—whatever your heart desires. Other people choose to sing for the same reason. It doesn't matter if you have a "good" singing voice or not. If you use your voice joyfully, passionately, and to uplift yourself and others, then you are truly utilizing your creative power in a positive way through sound. Music, words, and other sounds we create with our voices, bodies, or instruments, have the ability to profoundly affect our emotions and our moods.

Listen carefully to earth's music: wind, rain, birds, insects. Many Native American cultures believe that the very soil beneath our feet is telling us something, if we would only listen. The more you open your ears to the sounds of the earth, the more connected you become to Her. In fact, all of our senses, the links to our environment, have the ability to trigger our deepest, most private emotions. What do you do when a sound, or a smell, triggers a bad memory? The first thing to do is this: understand that your reaction is normal. Embrace it and use it as an opportunity to learn more about yourself.

The Mother and Child Reunion:
Your True Relationship with the Earth

Recall a time, possibly in early childhood, when you felt a connection with nature. You may not have understood this connection because to the very young, such things are often experienced as rather ordinary. As children, we are closer to the earth, literally and figuratively. It's only as we get older and taller that our hearts, and minds, grow further from the earth. Perhaps this is how, in time, we forget where we come from and put our relationship to nature on the back burner.

My friend Libby and I used to climb plum trees, eat the fruit, and chat all afternoon during the summer. We didn't worry about the things adults worry about, like the fruit being dirty. Now that I'm an adult, I'd probably go inside and wash the plums, for fear that they are wormy, or have tiny bits of bug poo on them. As kids, we pick fruit, wipe it on our t-shirts (maybe), and munch away. Libby and I regularly shared nature's wonders: we played in the rain, ran in the wind, soaked up the sun, climbed trees and rocks, and fed small animals together. She was my earth sister.

Many years later, she is miraculously unchanged in her love of animals and her respect for nature. To live in consciousness of Mother Earth, and all of the life that She sustains, is a choice that can be made now. When I asked a four-year-old where monkeys come from, he replied, "The cage at the zoo." In our fast-paced, technology-driven society, this lack of awareness is not even a tiny blip on our concern-radar. I challenge everyone who reads this to take the time to reconnect to Nature.

Write down your fondest, or most vivid, memory about nature. It can be as simple as watching a butterfly, or as adventurous as riding a horse across a stream. Write all of the details that you recall, including where you were, what colors or smells you remember, and how you felt at the time. Is it possible to recreate the experience? If so, commit to doing it! If it's not possible to recreate that experience, then go out and discover the natural world again, as though it were the very first time.

Draw a flower that is still alive and growing. As your eyes follow the curve of the stem and the curl of the petal, let your pencil flow at a leisurely pace. Don't rush yourself! Even if your "flower" is really a weed, try to capture its unique beauty as seen through only your eyes. We are all artists. As I always say, I may not be Michelangelo, but neither was Monet!

Our senses are naturally-occurring phenomena. We have them all of our lives, from birth to death, if we are lucky. So how is it that we grow to take our senses for granted? We get caught up in the day-to-day hassles of life.

As young women, we are also distracted by the need to protect ourselves physically and emotionally; the desire to please and be accepted by others; and just figuring out who we really are on the inside. Why do we not take time to acknowledge what is always there?

Putting gratitude in your attitude can at first be like pulling teeth. Eventually, it will become second nature.

4.

Chapter Four:

Identifying and Overcoming Spiritual Blocks

"It's not the load that breaks you down, it's the way you carry it. —Lena Horne

Jenny's Story

Jenny, a timid 16-year-old, told me, "My fears control me. Sometimes, I feel like I'm afraid of everything."

"What is your biggest fear?" I asked.

She thought a moment, then said, "I'm afraid of being good for nothing."

When I asked her to explain she said, "I've always been told I can't do anything right. My grades aren't good enough. My friends aren't good enough. I could do better if I wasn't so lazy, thoughtless, or distracted by dumb TV shows. So I'll never really be good at anything, and I'll always fail if I try." She paused a moment and began chewing on a fingernail. "Things in life are too hard, and I just don't have what it takes to really make it in the world. So how is my life even worth anything? I mean, why am I here? Am I just wasting space?"

I replied, "If your fear of being good for nothing had a name, what would it be?"

She looked at me with a puzzled expression and said, "I just told you. It's *fear*."

"No, a name, just like a person," I said.

She smiled and said, "*Jackass*." I learned much later that this was a name used frequently in her home by her parents to refer to Jenny or her brother; then, later, by her brother to refer to her.

"O.K., let's call him Jack for short. When is Jack happy? When does he thrive and grow?" I asked.

"When I stop myself from trying something new because I think I'll mess up," Jenny replied.

"When was the last time that happened?" I asked.

"When I wanted to join in on that dance project with the other girls," she answered. "I knew I would be too slow, or just look stupid. So I sat on the floor, and watched them dance."

"How did that feel?" I asked.

"I was kinda sad because I was on the floor instead of dancing, but listening to the music was cool," she said.

"It sounds like the music made you feel a little better," I said.

She agreed. "Much. I started to just chill out and watch them practice. I was telling the other girls that they looked good, and that they were really doing a great job."

"It sounds to me like Jack went away," I said.

She laughed and said, "I guess he doesn't like music."

I thought to myself, *I think she has something there.* We decided to do an experiment. Every time Jenny was afraid to try something new, she would play music while thinking about the fear. If "Jack" was particularly obnoxious that day, she would play a CD by her favorite group, Blink 182. Shocker of shockers, Jack *hated* that group! We discovered in time that there were lots of things Jack hated—nutritious foods, laughter, when Jenny got good grades in school, when a friend said something sweet. Now, how do you like that? When Jenny felt low, Jack was always there to keep her company! But whenever she felt like she had accomplished something, he was nowhere to be found! He deserted her! Jenny soon found many ways to keep Jack in his place. She learned how to honor her creative spirit, squash her self-doubts, and to not be so afraid of making mistakes. The last I heard, Jack was still alive, but he had moved far, far away, to a very remote location. Somewhere unreachable by telephone.

It is an act of profound courage to confront your fears. For many young women, even admitting their fears is so hard that they never speak of them to anyone. Sometimes, letting go of fear is a *process.* In this case, take "baby steps," like writing one sentence in your journal pertaining to your fear, then putting your journal away. Take it out again the next time you feel ready to write another sentence. Read what you have written from time to time. You may feel your reaction to the fear change the more you read about it, or the more you write about it. If you discover that the fear seems to be lessening over time, you may be becoming "desensitized" to it.

In other words, confronting it over and over again may make it seem less frightening. Of course, this does not always happen. If you find that thinking about or writing about your fear only makes it worse, or causes you extreme anxiety (nightmares, jitters, panic, loss of appetite), then I again strongly suggest you talk to a mental health professional. People like therapists and counselors can usually keep your conversations confidential **unless** they determine that you are a great risk to yourself or someone else. They are obligated, morally and legally, to do what is necessary to protect you and the public. If you have concerns about confidentiality, discuss it with the counselor, and he or she can explain their policy.

Above all, remember that it is your right to speak your feelings out loud, and to share your experiences with another person in a trusting, non-judgmental atmosphere.

Resentment

Holding on to resentment can crush your resolve to follow a spiritual path as well as breed bitterness and contempt. You may have every reason to be angry, hurt, and even want revenge on people who have hurt you, but these feelings can turn on you, and poison you to the light, or good, in people. I am a firm believer that despite what the media portrays, there are more good people in the world than bad people. However, being physically abused, emotionally battered, sexually harassed, or sexually violated can cause us to throw up permanent blocks against the evil in the world, invariably also shielding us from the beauty and light. These are called "defense mechanisms," and our subconscious has designed them to protect us from further emotional pain. At some point, we need protection from our protection—the defense mechanisms can start to rule our lives. Good people may want to befriend us, but our walls shut them out. Opportunities can come our way, but bitterness holds us back, mocking us with, "You aren't good enough." But don't despair, Spirited One! You have three priceless tools that will carry you through the challenges of resentment: *Acceptance*, *Forgiveness*, and *Courage*.

Why, you may ask, should I, or anyone, just *accept* the pain and victimization that's been inflicted on me? Well, as we've seen recently on the news and all over social media with the "Me Too" movement regarding sexual harassment and assault, women have always had valid reasons for "accepting" abuse or keeping quiet. The women in Hollywood who brought this movement to the forefront shed light on a fact that has always existed since women decided to make their own way in the careers of their choice: it doesn't matter who you are, what you look like, how old you are, or what your profession is, you are likely to experience some form of unwanted sexual attention in your lifetime. It can be verbal or physical, overtly threatening or subtle, but the message gets across that you are expected to take it if you want to keep your job. What we are now seeing, due to the bravery of women coming forward by the thousands to say "No more!" to being treated this way, is that acceptance does not mean that you are rolling over and letting people wipe their feet on you. On the contrary, acceptance means reclaiming your power and taking ownership of your life. Without even meaning to, these women in Hollywood reclaiming their power have inspired women all over the world to also reclaim theirs. It is a magnificent time to be a girl in this age of reclaiming our power, reclaiming our time (as the great Congresswoman Maxine Waters says), and embracing our strength.

I have often heard people say, "Now that I am an adult, I can finally allow myself to feel angry towards the people that hurt me. I can now move on with my life." Or, "I can now take care of my inner child." What if your inner child is also your outer child? I mean, *what if you actually ARE a child*? Personally, I do not believe that a person should wait until the age of 18 to feel anger! It is unfortunate and unfair that some girls will have to think about taking back their power, or taking responsibility for their safety, at an absurdly early age. Youth is the time when all people should feel safe, protected, loved, and free; not full of anger. The truth is, the feeling of anger is often there, but the feeling of safety is not—it can feel very unsafe to honor your anger, privately, or to use your voice and share it. This is especially true when you are currently in an abusive situation. It is imperative that you put your safety and well-being first, and that means being heard.

What about the saying "Forgive and forget?" You are not going to forget the impact that your pain has had on your life. You may never forget the person or persons that caused you pain, or the circumstances that led to your unusually challenging life. But *forgiveness* is more for you than for the people that hurt you. You cannot truly move forward without forgiveness; you will be held in the grasp of bitterness and regret. Forgive those people who have hurt you, forgive yourself if you blame yourself for any of your pain, learn the lessons that your challenges are meant to teach you, and move on with your life. Spirituality and resentment never go hand in hand. You have the power to control how your pain manifests itself within your spirit. It's not easy, but you will be rewarded with peace and growth.

Releasing your pain means reliving it, and opening up can be scary. This is where your *courage* comes in. By simply living your life, standing up for yourself and your values, transcending your experiences, and connecting to your spirit, you have already proven that you are a courageous young woman. Your courage will see you through the difficult process of seeking help from others. You will likely encounter obstacles, but you must insist on being heard. You are important, and so is your healing.

Shame

It is common to feel shame for bad things that have happened to you, as well as your own negative behaviors. If you are doing something that you know is wrong, or living a lifestyle that you aren't proud of, ask yourself why: "Why do I steal?" "Why do I do drugs?" "Why am I sexually promiscuous?" Ask yourself how it makes you feel to do these things. Remember, some things that we do can make us feel good, even giddy, in the moment. If I steal a shirt from my favorite store, I might feel a rush of excitement, or a thrill knowing that I got away with something. Your spiritual voice comes in when something inside you says, "Are you proud of yourself right now? Do you really want to be that type of person?" Maybe you say to yourself, "Darn right I do! I have a new shirt, it was free, and it looks great on me!"

Understand that this behavior is not who you really are. It is your dark side (we all have one) getting over on your good, "light" side. The dark side tells you that you are not worthy of goodness, that you are not capable of making the right choices, and that you are not good enough to live honestly and authentically. The shame robs you of your right to feel pride in being the young, glorious goddess that you are. Bad things happen to us, and sometimes we turn around and do other bad things, keeping the cycle of shame going full throttle.

It is especially devastating when someone that we love and trust violates our trust. This can even make us feel guilty, like, "How could I have been so stupid to trust that person? Why didn't I see them for who they really are?" We punish ourselves, beat up on ourselves, feel crappy, engage in reckless behavior trying to make up for our past mistakes, get hurt, feel guilty, punish ourselves...do you see the pattern?

In fact, mistakes are no mistake; they are experiences that are valuable learning tools, but that we don't wish to repeat. You are ultimately responsible for your choices, and you already possess all the heart, strength, and intelligence that you need to make those choices.

The only thing that may be missing is the wisdom that only age and experience can provide. If you don't have decades of wisdom behind you, your choices have to come from another source. When there is a choice to be made, don't ignore your intuition. Intuition is like the voice of your Higher Power trying to steer you in the right direction. Humans are the only animals that regularly question their intuition, or instincts, especially when it comes to other humans. We don't trust ourselves!

Oprah has said on her TV show, "When you see crazy coming, cross the street." Well, sometimes, we women see "crazy" coming, and say, "Hey, Crazy! Over here! Want to come to my house?" As girls and young women, we have a tendency to trust blindly and without reason. We get caught up in romanticism and fantasies, and not just where love interests are concerned. We do the same thing with our girl friends, often because we crave connections. Sometimes we have healthy, supportive friendships with responsible people. Other times we have friendships that are not true friendships: our "friends" put us down and pretend they're "joking," or encourage us to do stupid or dangerous things.

I remember an incident that happened when I was 17 where I didn't listen to my intuition, and later regretted it. I was in a 2-seater sports car with my boyfriend,

James, and one of his friends was driving. He was a little older than us, probably 20, and had a really nice car. The problems were that he was intoxicated, driving at least 100 miles per hour, and I was sitting on James's lap because, like I said, it was a 2-seater car. I was scared half out of my mind that we would have an accident. If we had, there would be little chance that any of us would survive, especially going as fast as we were. My mind kept screaming at me to say something, to ask the driver to slow down, to let me out of the car...*something*, but for some reason, I said nothing. Of course, now I know that it wasn't just "my mind" screaming at me, but my intuition, the voice of my Higher Power, telling me to get the heck out of that car.

What insanity would compel a young girl with her whole life ahead of her to keep quiet in such a dangerous situation? Well, like many girls, I was able to talk myself out of self-care. "I'm exaggerating the problem. He knows what he's doing. He can handle his own car. If there was a risk, James would tell him to slow down. I'll look like a baby. I'll look stupid. This guy will talk about me later to my friends. He won't like me." And so on, and so on.

The reason I regretted my decision to keep quiet is this: as I later pondered what had happened, it struck me that all the acceptance in the world would be of little comfort to me if I was dead. All of the necessary elements of danger were present: alcohol, stupidity, speed, and, thanks to me, silence. Every single time I hear about a deadly crash involving high speeds and alcohol, I thank God that I lived to tell my own story.

Now, I would get out of a car and take my chances of catching a cab (a good reason to always have your own money with you), a bus, a Lyft or Uber, or even call the police for help, rather than risk life and limb just so someone I barely know won't think I'm lame. The truth is, you are less likely to follow others in the wrong direction if you are following your own spiritual path. You will listen to your Higher Power when it tries to guide you, and you will not disregard your inner voice when it's trying to be heard. The *real* you, the light side that is stronger than the dark side, is trustworthy and wise. So is your Higher Power. Believe in yourself, know that you are blessed and worthy of the blessings, and you will be triumphant!

Jealousy

Jealousy is a colossal waste of time. Jealous people tend to exude an ugly energy that can hover like a black cloud. Of course, we've all been jealous of someone else, often starting in early childhood. My first clear memory of jealousy goes back to the second grade when Lola came to my school. At the tender age of six, I literally seethed with green envy as I stared at the back of her head. She had super long, curly hair in braids, and I used to pull them from my seat behind her. She would sit, remarkably composed for a seven-year-old, and quietly take my torture like a champ. She had a glamorous, well-dressed mom who was a charming man-magnet. Darling little thing that I was, I spoke badly about Lola, calling her conceited, bony, stuck-up, etc., etc., etc. As fate would have it, our mothers became fast friends. We grew up like sisters, being the only children of divorced moms. Ultimately, I realized two things: 1) I was actually trying to get her attention and 2) my jealousy said more about me than it did about her.

As the years passed, I became intensely aware of blessings in my own life that she missed in hers; for example, my father was a big part of my life, and she did not have a father growing up. Still, like sisters, we loved each other, but fought like cats and dogs. My friendship with Lola was my first lesson in understanding that different people have different lives, complete with their own unique sets of blessings and challenges. At my wedding, Lola told my father how much she had looked up to him as a child, and it reminded me, yet again, to send up a prayer of thanks.

When we focus on other people's fortunes instead of our own, we deny ourselves the self-love and attention we need. We get into the habit of looking outside of ourselves rather than within ourselves. We unknowingly seek sadness and malcontent by wanting someone else's stuff, boyfriend or girlfriend, house, popularity, or whatever. Instead of healing ourselves, jealousy causes us to hurt ourselves mentally and emotionally. Instead of living our own lives, we live outside of our lives focusing on what we *perceive* is someone else's charmed existence. Perceptions are like reflections in a mirror—they appear to be accurate representations of an image, but there are slight distortions that can't be easily seen with the naked eye.

You'd be surprised at how many beautiful, popular, perfect-looking girls are insecure, frightened people. I wish that were not the case, but often it is. Many girls feel a lot of pressure to maintain a perfect façade, which is one thing that leads to eating disorders. Maybe the flawless Wonder Girl that incurs your jealous wrath is a happy, secure, loved, rich, shiny-tressed dream fairy with a 4.0 GPA. So what? Would you honestly be happier if she went home every day to a mud hut where she threw herself in tears upon a flat, hard mattress and took orders from her evil stepmother before sitting down to a dinner of cold porridge?

Try this exercise: look in the mirror and say out loud, "I HATE her! She thinks she's so hot, the stuck-up cow!" Notice what your facial expression is when you say this. Now say out loud, "Wow! It's so cool that she got a full scholarship to Harvard right after winning the Miss Teen America pageant! I'm very happy for her!" How does your facial expression differ now from before? How does your body feel?

Studies prove that smiling is not only emotionally better for you than frowning, but also physically healthier, and can even prolong your life. So maybe you can't help the occasional twinge of jealousy, but try to push it aside. It will do you more harm than good. If you sincerely hope the best for other people, and even send those people positive thoughts and blessings, you are making yourself a source of warm, loving energy in the world. You will attract people who are heart-centered, honest, and good.

This magical, nurturing, healing power is one of woman's greatest gifts. We can call forth warmth and love where before there was none. Women of all ages, from all backgrounds, are changing the world because they have love in their hearts. If more women were taught to support and encourage each other at a very young age, instead of being fanatically competitive, imagine how much more dynamic we would be!

Ingratitude

Ingratitude is a steadfast spiritual block. It seems so harmless, and that's what makes it so dangerous. It may seem like it's not a big deal to ignore the good things in life, especially since for many girls, there are so many bad things. You may think, *How can I be expected to be grateful when my life is so hard?* There are days when it takes much creative thinking to find something to be grateful for. It's always hardest during times of suffering, when everything seems hopeless. But for girls who are lucky enough to live in the U.S., there are resources available to us that are not available to most of the girls in the world.

We are the luckiest females on earth because while others fight for the right to an education, it is required for the American girl. It is *against the law* to not educate an American child. We also have free health care until the age of eighteen, lots of available mental health services, and community-based services that millions of people around the world only dream about. When it feels like there is nothing to be grateful for, think of the one thing that you have for sure: *life*. Life is the greatest gift of all, and as long as you have that, there is always hope for the future.

5.

Chapter Five:
Groups and Rituals

"This is the power of gathering: it inspires us to be more hopeful, more joyful, more thoughtful. In a word, more alive."—Alice Walker

What greater reward is there than to be a link in a chain of healing? Being able to help others and learning to willingly accept feedback and support, are good reasons to belong to a spirituality group. You may even want to start one of your own. It may seem daunting, but it's not as hard as you may think. One of my friends loves to read, so she put the word out that she was starting a book club. It's as simple as that. Some people want to lose weight, so they join groups like Weight Watchers, where like-minded people with similar goals and similar struggles can meet. All types of groups hold discussions about what they are doing to meet their goals, where they are slipping up, and what they feel they need to work on to make their journey easier.

The reasons why people decide to join groups vary. As with spirituality groups, the common thread of most women's groups is a desire to join with other women in an atmosphere of acceptance, comfort, and fun. Some groups end up giving much more than was expected. I once read a story about a woman who joined a knitting circle shortly after the sudden death of her child. The woman poignantly wrote of how she slowly began to mend her broken heart with the steady rhythm of her fingers, the creative outlet that knitting provided, and the camaraderie of the women in her circle. Your needs can be met if you create the type of group that you would want to join, or you can find a group by asking around or doing a little research. Are you interested in learning about different spiritual philosophies? Have you started on your path, but find yourself stuck in a rut and don't know how to move forward? Do you simply want a group of people to pray or meditate with? Are you completely clueless about spirituality and just want to indulge your curiosity? As you are looking for a group, remember that for many people, spirituality goes hand in hand with religion. If this is not the case for you, finding a group that is not based in a specific religion may complicate your search somewhat, but keep looking. You may want to ask a clergy person for ideas or call a local counseling center. Many counseling centers have spirituality groups or can provide referrals. Try to be as specific as possible about what you want in a group. Do you remember the exercise in Chapter 1 where you pointed out the kind of people you want in your life? The same idea applies when you think of your group members. However, there are additional qualities in a group member that are non-negotiable: patience, a willingness to keep confidences, and a non-judgmental personality. Not every person is going to think the same or be on the same path. That is one of the interesting things about being in a group. Diversity automatically creates a learning environment.

Young people are very vulnerable to cults and manipulative groups of people with a negative agenda, so be very careful with whom you get involved! Stick with people close to your own age group and beware of people who seem to be recruiting, or who come on strong. Religious and spiritual cults are just as dangerous as gangs, and they come in every variety. Keep an eye out for people who offer unconditional love as soon as you meet them, housing, food, and a "family" atmosphere, or who want all of your time. Definitely run from people who ask you for money. Cultists are not necessarily kooks wearing sandwich boards, or odd-looking people in weird clothes. You know what they say about dangerous people: they look just like you and me. Don't ignore your instincts when someone gives you the creeps. As I've said before, those feelings are there for a reason: to keep you safe.

I may have sufficiently scared the crap out of you now, but all of the warnings are meant to help you stay safe and aware.

Snippets about Religions

Remember how I mentioned in the Introduction that we would briefly discuss religion? Well here we are. I want to point out that I am not a theologian, nor am I any type of expert on religion. Personally, I was baptized and raised as a Catholic, and remain one to this day. However, many would consider me to be a very "liberal" Catholic, or possibly a Unitarian (more on that later). I enjoy studying all cultures and religions of the world, if for no other reason than curiosity. I believe in God, and I believe that Jesus Christ was the Son of God, but I also believe that the Buddha was more than just your average bald guy in a toga. I have an attitude about different religions and spiritual belief systems that works for me, and it includes respect for the traditions of other people. As the Dalai Lama wrote, "I believe it is essential that we extend our understanding of each other's spiritual practices and prayers. This is not necessarily in order that we can adopt them ourselves, but because to do so increases our opportunities for mutual respect. Sometimes, too, we encounter something in another tradition that helps us better appreciate something in our own." I adopt ideas from various beliefs and apply them to my own life, my behavior, and my treatment of others. The wonderful thing is, most of the major religions of the world share many of the same beliefs. Does that surprise you? When we consider the centuries of war, pain, and strife inflicted on the world in the name of religion, it's tragically ironic that believers share so many commonalities. For example, the Law of Karma originated in Eastern religions, most notably, Hinduism, but the Christian, or biblical, version of this concept is "What a man sows, he must reap," and the Pagan (i.e., Wiccan) version of this is the Threefold Law, which states that whatever acts you commit on the world, good or bad, will come back to you threefold. Unitarianism, a belief system based on both Christian and Jewish teachings, also draws from spiritual teachings of the earth-centered traditions, such as Wicca. So we aren't necessarily as different as we think, or as we are led to believe. Of course, there are plenty of exceptions, but you can come to those conclusions on your own. Here is a quick overview of some religions and systems of belief. Keep in mind, the intricacies of these religions are incredibly vast. In other words, the stuff I'm leaving out could fill volumes. If you have any questions, conduct your own research, and be ready to find hundreds of opinions on each and every subject.

Atheism: Having no belief in the existence of God or gods. For followers of Agnosticism, a close relation to Atheism, humans do not know for sure whether God or gods exist and for some Agnostics, humans can never know.

Bahai: A new religion established approximately 150 years ago. It is a worldwide religion based on the teachings of Baha'u'llah (1817–1892). He stated that people should put aside their differences and unite on the basis of his teachings. Baha'u'llah preached the eradication of different religions and races so that all people could unite as one family.

Buddhism: Based on the teachings of Siddartha Gautama (known as the *Buddha*). These teachings center around his key discoveries, known as the Four Noble Truths: *dukkha* (suffering), *tanha* (personal desire), overcoming *tanha* (you must overcome the traps of self-interest or desire), and *The Eightfold Path* (the way to overcome *tanha*). Buddhism is very complex, and also includes basic principles, one of which is *karma*.

Catholicism, or Roman Catholicism: One of the three great branches of Christianity. God came to earth represented by his Son, Jesus Christ, to teach people how to live in this world so that they can get to the next world and experience eternal life. The Church itself provides the Sacraments which help Catholics live their lives appropriately. The Sacraments are *baptism,* *confirmation, holy matrimony* (marriage) or *holy orders* (dedication of one's life to God, as opposed to another person, as in marriage), and *sacrament of the sick* (often referred to as last rites when one is preparing to die). Throughout life, the recurring Sacraments are *confession* and *mass*.

Christianity: The most widespread of the world's religions, with the most followers. Based on the life and teachings of Jesus. Jesus preached peace, love and compassion, and disregarded the social barriers that were the norm of His time, which kept people separate and categorized. This led to Jesus being charged with treason and executed.

Church of Jesus Christ of Latter-Day Saints (Mormonism): Founded by Joseph Smith, based in Salt Lake City, Utah. The Father (Elohim) and the Son (Jesus, who became the God of Israel, Jehovah) appeared to Smith, instructing him to restore the true Church. God was once a man, then exalted to Godhood. He and his heavenly wife had billions of spirit children, the first of whom was Jesus and became a God while only a spirit. The rebellious spirit children were led by Lucifer, and the non-rebellious children became humans, who could earn Godhood through strict adherence and obedience to the gospel.

Church of Scientology: Founded by L. Ron Hubbard (the author of *Dianetics*). This religion has gained much media attention due to the number of celebrities that follow it, including Tom Cruise and John Travolta. Humans are immortal spiritual beings who will experience ongoing life through reincarnation. A human has unlimited capabilities, but they are imprisoned by matter, energy, space, and time (MEST). Salvation is the recovery of spiritual freedom and the god-like ability to control MEST.

Eastern Orthodoxy: Also one of the three branches of Christianity. They practice the one true Christian faith, passed down by sacred tradition. They don't follow the Pope, but instead follow the Ecumenical Patriarch, who is currently Bartholomew I.

Hinduism: A major world religion that originated from the ancient religions of India. The ancient gods (especially Brahma, Vishnu, and Shiva) represent various aspects of the divine. As is common to many religions, the ultimate goal is oneness with the divine (called *Brahman*), which is a state known as *Nirvana*. Nirvana can be achieved through reincarnation according to the law of karma.

Islam: The second largest world religion, and the third largest in America. Islam is an Arabic word that means "submission to the will of God." It is based on the teachings of Muhammad, who is considered to be the greatest prophet. Followers are called Muslims. Muslims observe the *Five Pillars*, which are reciting "there is no God but Allah and Muhammad is his messenger," praying five times a day, fasting, giving donations (*alms*) to the poor, and going on a pilgrimage to Mecca.

Judaism: This religion originated with God's call to Abraham to be the father of a great people whose destiny was to inherit the land of Canaan. The foundation of Judaism is the Torah, which is made up of the books Genesis through Deuteronomy, and tells of the Israelites' bondage in Egypt all the way through the giving of the Law through Moses. The three branches of modern Judaism are Orthodox (literal adherence to the tenets of the Torah as interpreted by the Talmud), Conservative (middle-ground traditionalism), and Reform (liberal, often with a greater emphasis on Jewish culture).

Paganism (see Wicca): An earth-based, polytheistic (many gods) religion with ancient roots. Women and men are of equal importance, and goddess worship is prevalent. Paganism emphasizes recognition of the divine in nature.

Protestantism: One of the three branches of Christianity. Everyone is fallible, and therefore, Protestants don't rely on a set doctrine or the Pope's leadership, as that too has the potential to be fallible.

Santeria: The literal translation is "worship of the saints." Combines Catholicism and traditional African religions that came into being when African slaves were brought to the Caribbean.

Shamanism: The spiritual view of Native American, and other early cultures. "Shamans" (often referred to as spiritual leaders or *witch doctors*) can heal and help guide believers. They are known to enter altered states of consciousness either naturally, or with the assistance of mind-altering natural herbs or drugs.

Sikhism: Combining aspects of Hinduism and Islam, this religion has its roots in India. Based on the teachings of its founder, Nanak, in the 15th century A.D. Followers are called Sikhs and worship one God named Sat Nam (which means "True Name"). The ultimate goal is to merge with the "universal force."

Watchtower Bible and Tract Society (Jehovah's Witnesses): God's real name is "Jehovah." Jesus is "a god," not *God*. Only 144,000 people will go to heaven. Other faithful followers will enjoy eternity on earth, which will be a paradise. The "lost," or non-believers, will face annihilation.

Wicca: Also known as witchcraft, it's a pagan, earth-centered religion that includes the worship of pre-Christian gods and goddesses. In congruence with the Threefold Law, a common principle is "Do what you will, and harm none." Wiccans hold nature and Mother Earth in high regard.

The Amish and Quakers deserve honorable mention here, though they are not technically part of any "religion." They exist in faith-based communities with their basis in Christianity.

Amish: The Amish are often identified by their traditional style of dress, which is very modest and simple. However, they are Protestant Christians who prioritize community, pacifism, and separation from the modern world.

Quakers: Also referred to as the Society of Friends, or "Friends," Quakers are pacifists who choose a life of simplicity and community. Unlike the Amish, they live in the modern world in diverse communities. They are Protestant Christians without a specific doctrine or creed; direct communion with God and meditation is the core of their belief.

Prayers

It is a myth that praying is only for religious people. Prayer can be as simple as communing with nature. You can pray while you are meditating, walking, shopping, or driving. There are no rules to prayer! According to the book *Eight Sacred Horizons: The Religious Imagination East to West,* "Prayer is any personal, impersonal, or transpersonal way to express communion with the sacred." However, prayer, like spirituality, is personal, and can be designed and defined by you.

Some of the benefits of prayer include:

* Emotional healing.

* Opening your heart to receive guidance from your Higher Power.

* Voicing your needs and wants.

* Building a bridge to your imaginative and creative self.

Prayer is also a good way to tackle the nasty residue left by a mean person. You can pray for them, or simply send them positive energy during an everyday activity. It is impossible to change someone else's behavior, but that is where the power of your prayers comes in. While others may never change, prayer can help you view their effect on you differently. Prayer, like affirmations, puts positive energy out into the universe, if used with a pure heart and good intentions. Even if you don't believe in "God" or a Higher Power, there is nothing stopping you from being a conduit of love, peace, and joy. You don't have to put a name to the "person" you are praying to, even though that is a customary practice. Many Catholics pray to saints, as well as God, Mary the Holy Mother, and Jesus. This type of prayer works for some people, and not for others. That doesn't mean that one way is better, or more effective, than the other. The power of your prayers may surprise you. You can ask God, the universe, or whomever, for whatever you want, and be careful—you just may get it. I used to think that prayer for personal gain was somehow sinful or selfish, but now I feel differently.

Once, after choir practice, some members of my choir were holding a prayer circle. I told my friend Francie, "I am so broke right now. I sure wish I could pray for some money!"

"You can pray for money," she said.

I was stunned. "I can?" I asked.

"Sure you can. Why not?" she said.

"Isn't it greedy to ask for money?" I asked.

"Just like everything else, if you need it, you might as well pray on it. It certainly can't hurt. You're already broke," she replied.

She did have a point, so during circle I said out loud, "I am seriously poor right now. This week, I need my blessings to be financial!" My prayer was fervent and sincere—I mean, it's not like I was planning to buy something illegal; I had bills to pay. Later that month, I got an unexpected financial windfall! And, ironically, that windfall benefitted Francie, too: she was moving out of town for a fantastic job opportunity and didn't have enough money to move. I loaned her the money, she moved, and I had enough money to pay my bills (and of course, buy a cute pair of shoes).

Prayer can be used to send up thanks, also. I've spent a lot of time talking about appreciating the blessings that life has bestowed upon us, even if the most obvious blessing is that we are alive. If you give it some thought, I'm sure you'll find at least a couple of blessings every single day. Why not thank your Higher Power for your daily blessings? It needn't be a big production; you can say "Thanks" with a shout or with a whisper, but being thankful has the same benefits for your spiritual and emotional health as smiling, laughing, or eating chocolate.

6.

Chapter Six:

Using Love and Compassion as Spiritual Catalysts

"Everyone has the power for greatness, not for fame but greatness, because greatness is determined by service."—Martin Luther King, Jr.

Greatness in Service

I once decided on compassion as a spirituality group topic and have since discussed compassion with countless teens. Depending on their personal experiences, these girls' views on compassion differed greatly. Some of them thought of compassion as a service, something you do, and then it's over. One teen told of her family's ritual of feeding the homeless at a shelter every Thanksgiving. For another girl, a 12-year-old Catholic, compassion was volunteer work she was expected to do for her Confirmation (a Catholic sacrament). Many of these troubled girls described a life of what they perceived as independence, but was really isolation, loneliness, and lack of purpose. The deep anger and hurt that resulted from not receiving compassion when they needed it most shut them down emotionally. They did not see this defense mechanism as a problem, but as a survival tool.

People who only focus on themselves and their own issues do so because they think that this is the way to solve their problems and eventually be happy. But these people aren't usually happy, not that real, truly peaceful happiness that we all yearn for. You know why?

Because *nobody likes them*! People may tolerate selfishness, but nobody likes a selfish person. And be honest: can you really be happy if people don't like you? I'm not saying that we should practice compassion only to be liked. Fake compassion is as transparent as glass. On a recent episode of TV's "South Park" (What? I'm only supposed to quote spiritual leaders?) a kid named Cartman pretended to care about his friend Kyle only to be invited to Kyle's big birthday party. He was kind and sweet towards Kyle, which was highly unusual. Cartman gave Kyle a birthday present, humbly acting as though it was out of genuine friendship. Secretly, he even locked up another kid for a week so he could take that kid's place at the party! Granted, Cartman got what he wanted in the end, but everyone found out that he was a lying, manipulative jerk that couldn't be trusted. The moral of this deep and profound story? It's a trade-off—you can selfishly step on people to get what you want, but you will lose respect, trust, and friendships. You may get instant gratification, but your spirit will suffer in the long run.

With our busy and over-scheduled lifestyles, you may think it would be hard to find opportunities to be compassionate. On the contrary, the more people you come in contact with, the more opportunities to express compassion. You don't have to send the amount of money you would spend on your daily trip to Starbucks to a person suffering or starving in a third world country, but still, every single day, you can change someone's life. Do you know how powerful that is? Even if you smile at someone who looks like they are having a bad day, or let another driver get in front of you in a traffic jam, or help an elderly lady reach something in the grocery store, you are practicing great acts of compassion.

Imagine a man just lost his wife of many years. He spends his mornings on the couch watching TV and drinking coffee, remembering how much tastier his wife's coffee was. He goes to the grocery store weekly, a fairly unfamiliar place since his wife did the shopping all 50 years of their marriage. His children, some of whom live in another state, rarely have time for him because they are busy living their own lives and having their own children. Every day, he becomes more depressed.

One day, he is hanging out at the local senior center, where he joins in on the occasional card game. This is his only social outlet. Then, a young woman comes into the recreation hall, all smiles and boisterous activity. She goes from person to person, chatting, sometimes yelling into someone's hearing aid. As she makes her way towards him, he starts to perk up. He knows that she will engage him in a conversation, and they will end up laughing and talking about his days on the vaudeville circuit. That's when he met his wife, and it was the best time of his life. The girl sits down, patting him on the shoulder. They drink iced tea, and the old man becomes young again while she listens, on the edge of her seat, although she's heard this story a hundred times. She laughs at his jokes and asks him questions that she already knows the answers to. She tells him how exciting his stories are, and how lucky his grandchildren are to have him, so they can hear about his life as they get older. This girl doesn't realize it, but during the hour that she spends at the senior center, she has touched many lives profoundly, and given one old man reason to believe that he is not a burden, but an important person with a fascinating, educational history.

The story of the old man is not fictional. It is the true story of a man who was a favorite of one of my sacred girls, a girl with a tragic, violent history of her own. Helping the elderly was her way of getting outside of her problems and putting others first, even if only for a couple of hours a week. Did you know that you can literally save a life with a kind word, or a loving embrace? The young girl conversing with the old man is no more important than the person who helps the lady in the grocery store, or who smiles at the sad-looking stranger. We can each be a catalyst for change, and a conduit for love, in someone else's life. You may never know the significance of your kindness towards someone. Often, that's all people need: to know that they matter enough to someone, even a stranger, to get a few moments of blessed attention. The Dalai Lama said, "The moment you think only of yourself, the focus of your whole reality narrows, and because of this narrow focus, uncomfortable things can appear huge and bring you fear and discomfort and a sense of feeling overwhelmed by misery. The moment you think of others with a sense of caring, however, your view widens. Within that wider perspective, your own problems appear to be of little significance, and this makes a big difference."

None of this is to imply that instead of taking care of yourself, you should take care of only others. You can do both, and often caring for yourself and caring for others go hand in hand. If you can bring a smile, some peace, or a helping hand to someone, won't that make you feel all warm inside? At the very least, being available and present for another person will take your mind off of your own problems for a little while.

Predatory Girls

Predatory girls and their unfortunate quarry have always held a special place in my heart. When I was in the first grade, my predator was a girl named Flora. She stalked me practically every minute of the day at school. Like on that animal TV show "Jaws and Claws," I, her victim, always knew she was watching me, even when she skillfully hid herself. She could smell my fear. In my childish confusion, I didn't understand why I dreaded her presence, and yet played with her when she told me to, stole packets of sugar for her from the teacher's lounge, and let her cut me in line for everything from kickball to the bathroom.

A predatory girl is one who targets a particular girl as her victim. She is so focused on the discomfort of her prey that causing anxiety has been honed to an art form. Her single-minded determination to *take you down* takes bullying to dizzying new heights. The predatory girl is like the bully's bigger, meaner sister, and she sees herself as far more powerful than her victim. Sometimes, she disguises herself as a harmless peer, or maybe as a friend. But typically, she has no desire to toy with her victim's emotions. She doesn't like you, and she doesn't care who knows it.

It is a lucky girl who makes it to adulthood without ever having been the victim of a predatory girl. The sad fact is that most girls are aware of the predator in their midst, but they don't know what to do about it.

Fifteen-year-old Jeannine moaned about her predatory girl, "I tried everything! If I avoided her, she just showed up wherever I went. If I ignored her, that just pissed her off. If I smiled at her, she goes, 'why are you staring at me?'"

When I asked Jeannine how it ended, she said, "I still don't know. She, like, got bored with me, but she started picking on a friend of mine." She swept the back of her hand across her forehead, saying, "Phew! Thank God that's over!" with a big grin.

"But what about your friend? I asked.

She looked at me expressionlessly. "Well," she finally said, slowly, "it's not like it can last

forever."

Jeannine was dead wrong. The emotional and psychological scars can last forever, for the victim and her family. When I told my adult friends that I was writing about predatory girls, one friend said, "I can tell you all about that." The other women nodded their heads or rolled their eyes in understanding.

In talking with another friend, Kasy, I learned that a predator will use other people to strengthen the impact of their abuse. Kasy is a beautiful, 28-year-old woman who said that she was "tortured beyond belief" in junior high by one girl who "just would not stop." To add insult to injury, the predator enlisted the help of Kasy's younger sister Sophie. An odd turn of events happened after that: Sophie, who had never gotten along well with Kasy, suddenly began to be nice to her at home.

"It almost seems as if she wore herself out at school," Kasy said, "where she went out of her way to be my second worst enemy." The predator had a way of rewarding Sophie with

invitations to parties, trips to the mall with her clique, and cute gifts like bracelets and sunglasses. Sophie, Kasy sadly told me, had never seemed happier.

Why is it that girls are so mean to each other, generation after generation, that their behavior is portrayed in the media as being not exactly "normal," but definitely expected? Classic teen movies such as "Heathers," "Jawbreaker," "The Craft," and "Mean Girls" all portray girls as having an eerie capacity for true badness. Television has been showing us this for decades, from way back to when Nellie targeted Laura on "Little House on the Prairie" to reality TV's "Bad Girls Club." On the contrary, boys can generally be competitive, even aggressive, without causing quite as much damage to each other. We hear about tragedies like shootings in schools, churches, and movie theaters, where boys and young men who already had serious mental health issues finally snapped. These incidents are devastating, and thankfully, not a daily occurrence. The act of targeting innocents by predatory girls happens daily in schools across the country. It's no coincidence that this disparity between boys and girls leaks into almost every aspect of life, including diagnoses of depression. A recent study found that in 2002, 6.4% of U.S. girls (compared to 4.2% of U.S. boys) ages 15–18 were taking antidepressants. Girls also lead the pack in eating disorders and anxiety-related disorders. With all of the issues that their peers have to deal with, what is going on in the minds of predatory girls? In other words, what are they thinking? What can they possibly gain from targeting other girls? And more importantly, how can their victims deal with the pain so that it doesn't destroy them?

Girls who have been targeted by their peers, or victimized in some way, often have a heightened sense of imminent danger, and are reluctant to let down their walls. They feel if they aren't constantly on watch, looming over their feelings like a tower guard, they'll get hurt again. Of course, this might be true, but you can't avoid personal connections if you want to live an open, full life. You should never put up with being abused by anyone. You can protect yourself spiritually by utilizing tools such as meditation and journaling. Sharing your feelings with your friends can also help, but do not fall into the trap of "giving as good as you get." In other words, do not become a mirror of the destructive people that are hurting you. You want to rise above the muck, not wallow in the same garbage that inspires predatory girls. Be the better person, not by getting back at them, but by living your own life. There is a saying that goes, "The best revenge is living well." How true it is.

Blessing the Mean People

We've spent some time talking about compassion towards others. But what if the person in need of our compassion is just a jerk? Even predatory girls can really be hungry for our blessings. Praying for mean people, or even just sending positive thoughts their way, will never hurt you. You have probably heard, at some time in your life, that when someone is negative or nasty, it is usually because they have some sort of personal problem. This is probably true in many cases. In others, people are just creeps, and it is not your job to figure out why.

Dealing with jerks of all kinds is just a part of life, and there will always be situations where you'll get hurt. Trying to avoid pain entirely is like trying to avoid taxes; you might as well give it up and take the hit. Just like anger and stress, pain and frustration carry a level of energy that can either be crippling or dynamic. My friend Natalie's mom was deserted by her husband after 30 years of marriage. He left her for another woman. Nat's mom could barely get out of bed for months—she had never even had another boyfriend and had been with this guy since she was in high school. She finally pulled herself out of her slump, but continues to live in denial (15 years later!) that he'll come back to her. I'm no psychic, but I wouldn't put money on it.

A co-worker of mine, Mary Ann, went through a similar ordeal—after 26 years of marriage, her husband left her for her "best friend." This especially sucks, because she no longer had her friend's shoulder to cry on. However, she chose a radically different path than Nat's mom.

Of course, she was bitter and heartbroken, and performed some of the typical embarrassing antics that scorned people do: called him begging and crying, called her best friend and cussed her out, left nasty notes on both their cars. After about two weeks, though, she decided to harness the energy of her anger and direct it towards something positive for her. She took up kickboxing, which was a new craze at that time, and lost 30 pounds. She began painting again, a hobby that she had never found the time for while she was married, and received rave reviews for her beautiful portraits. One significant twist to this story is that before her divorce was final, her husband saw her at a gallery opening. Stunned by her toned biceps, sharp new haircut, funky highlights, and confident glow, he asked her if he could take her out on a date. She smiled sweetly and said, "No, thanks." She told me that she decided to let her pain drive her into self-improvement and self-affirmation, and she had literally never felt better.

When I went through my breakup, the one where I was going bald, I started dancing again, and did a lot of journaling. I mean, there are only so many bubble baths you can take before you have to rejoin the living! It is true empowerment when you channel your energy, even the negative energy, and recreate it to heal yourself. We all have the power to do this—with every piece of hurt, consciously create something else in your life to counteract it. Learn from your pain and use it to better yourself. That way, you have mastery over the problem, not the other way around.

Social Media

When I first got the idea for this book, social media did not yet exist. I know, it's hard to imagine a world without Instagram, Snapchat, Tumblr, and Facebook. Somehow, we survived. Don't get me wrong! I absolutely love social media. I hate to admit it, but it's where I get most of my daily news, keep up with distant relatives and friends, and share my life. Mostly, the good stuff in my life. And as crucial as social media seems to be in our daily lives, there are pros and cons to it.

Pros: you can get connected to your community; you can share artistic interests; you can share and discover music; you can learn how to do something new; you can keep up with friends and family; you can read news stories; you can watch cute animal videos; you can see and share cool food.

Cons: it encourages you to compare yourself to other people; it is rarely a reflection of others' reality; it may cause unhealthy levels of jealousy due to thinking those people actually live like that; it may encourage over-sharing that you will likely regret later, i.e., relationship drama, butt selfies, videos of you acting a fool, etc.; it may expose you to bullies, sexual predators, stalkers, and other dangerous types of people.

Social media should primarily be used in one of three ways: purely as entertainment, as a means to promote your business, and as a way to stay connected to people that you don't get to see very often. Please, think before you post. The hiring manager at your future dream job doesn't need to see your epic twerking skills when he or she researches you. And trust me, they will. Google is a mean, two-faced friend, long on memory and completely devoid of mercy. Remember—the internet is forever.

Karma: What Goes Around Comes Around

Maybe you've heard the word "karma" as in "It's bad karma to steal." Karma refers to action, or something you do, and there is good and bad karma. The basic law of karma is that your actions will eventually lead back to you, and you will be held responsible for what you've done. Don't worry, that includes the good stuff, too. However, these familiar phrases aren't just catchy little ditties:

What goes around comes around!

You reap what you sow!

For every action, there is an equal and opposite reaction!

If you can dish it out, you'd better be able to take it!

I'm rubber, you're glue...whatever you say bounces off of me and sticks back on you!

Oh, I could go on and on, but you get the gist. Virtually every spiritual tradition teaches that you get back what you put out there, whether good or bad. For example, true practitioners of Wicca do not use their craft as a means to inflict harm. The belief is that any hurtful energy that you put out will come back to you three times over. On the other hand, it is widely believed throughout the spiritual arena that good deeds will come back to you as well. Frankly, I'd rather spend my energy enjoying the fruits of my actions instead of dodging bad karma. Who needs the headache?

I'm not suggesting that you spend every second of your life working like a mule, performing good deeds, only so that you will reap worldly benefits. If your actions are fueled by selfishness, they will eventually backfire, as in the case of Cartman on "South Park." According to the Bhagavad Gita, an ancient Hindu text, selfless acts lead to spiritual blessings. Karma can turn into an endless cycle of egoism and greed if we constantly act with our own agenda in mind. It's very natural to think, "What am I going to get out of this?" Certainly, when I was a waitress, I thought of the tip I would receive if I was friendly, witty, and didn't spill food on my customers. I was young, and I was broke. I lived with three roommates and a pet rabbit in a roach-infested apartment in a sketchy neighborhood, so money was uppermost in my thoughts. I found myself getting really irritated if I worked hard to give great service and still got a lousy tip. At some point, I realized that some people are just bad tippers, and stopped taking it personally. If I relaxed and enjoyed myself, my smile wasn't "plastic," my shift felt shorter, and my customers were happier. Giving good service from the heart turned out to be rewarding, although not necessarily in a monetary way. I would willingly sacrifice more money, however, for contentment and peace, rather than to spend my 8-hour workday wishing I were somewhere else.

Love

About love...

It is possible to love and go about this process without loving; to love, and the act of loving, are two entirely different things.

You can say it: "Oh Baby, I love you!"

You can feel it: "I love him soooo much."

You can show it: "Darling, I cooked your favorite dinner. Can I rub your back? How was your day? Let me fluff your pillow."

But the big question is, can you do it? Remember, love is more than a beautiful word—it is also an action, a verb, an act, a series of actions and behaviors. Love is a willingness to grow, to change, to accept, to sacrifice, and to learn.

Can you feel vulnerable? Probably. But the real challenge is, can you be vulnerable? The act of existing in a state of vulnerability connotes a willingness to trust. This is the most difficult thing in the world to do. Can you open your heart, look deep inside yourself, and share your soul? This is trust. This is loving. To feel love is easy. To be in love is even easier. To say you love is easier than that. Don't ask yourself if you love. Challenge yourself and ask yourself if you are love-ing, if you are an active participant in this process. Ask yourself if you are giving. Ask yourself if you are open to receive what another has to offer. Ask yourself if you are loving yourself, truly loving yourself. This means feeding your soul, feeding your mind, nourishing your body, opening your heart even when it is hard to do, hugging yourself, smiling, laughing, being grateful for life, breathing, and sharing. It also means conquering the fear of feeling your true feelings, and bravely exploring what is really there. Begin the long journey of knowing yourself. If you are open to this journey, it will never end. Like any journey, there will be hills, valleys, and pitfalls. But do it anyway. Don't try it, do it. Give, and keep giving. Receive, and allow yourself an open heart. Love, and remember to motivate that love into action.

Be loving. Do love.

—*"One Page" essays*, December, 2000.

Write down the top five things you love about yourself. Read this list a few times, then write five more things. Ask yourself why you love these particular qualities. How does it make you feel when you read this list? The reason that I asked you to do this exercise is because it is necessary to be kind to yourself once in a while, to congratulate yourself, and to remind yourself of all the great things about you. If this is hard for you, make something up. You may be surprised to find that the lovable things you "fake" about yourself are, in reality, qualities that you actually do have. If not, ask yourself how you can become the person that you want to be. What steps would you need to take in order to meet your own "lovability quotient"? Because, when it comes right down to it, the power is within you to be a loving, caring person, and to fill your heart with love. I know that it's scary to open your heart if you've done it before and later regretted it. If you don't allow love back into your heart, you will miss out on life's greatest gift, and what I believe is truly the meaning of life: to love and be loved in return. I don't know which one feels better or is more healing to the soul.

It's no coincidence that many people who have survived a devastating illness, been the victim of a crime, or suffered a terrible loss, turn around and give support in the form of love and compassion to other people who have been through the same thing. Helping others is healing for the helper, so the act of giving can turn out to be a greater gift to ourselves. Many recovery programs, from drug rehabs to rape crisis centers, operate on the belief that reaching out to people in need is crucial to the healing process. In fact, many people find it satisfying to be able to give another person something that they themselves may have missed somewhere along the way: understanding, tenderness, acceptance, and patience. If the experiences are similar, it can be a way to revisit one's own pain and see a different conclusion to the story. Regardless of one's circumstances, however, compassion, altruism, and love have a funny way of making us feel hopeful, useful, and good. The spiritual benefits can even save your life, as they did for one of my sacred girls, a very troubled

17-year-old named Marisol. Her early childhood was full of betrayal and sexual abuse, but as a teen, she was able to turn her unmet need for effective parenting into a way to help the helpless.

As is often the case when a child is molested, Mari had serious problems as she got older. She joined a gang, started doing drugs, and spent time in juvie all before she was 15. She was also physically abused by all of her boyfriends. Mari's story could have ended in a number of unpleasant ways. She could have been killed by a rival gang. She could have died of a drug overdose. Luckily, she ended up in rehab and began to rebuild her life. Her recovery plan involved doing volunteer work at a nearby retirement home. Mari had always been a natural caregiver. Mari felt so good about her work with seniors that she often talked about them, relaying their life stories, laughing about how they responded to her bubbly, outrageous personality. She was able to take her painful experiences and transform her pain into a gift for loving and nurturing others in a way that she had never experienced herself. It took years of therapy, as well as help for her family, for the healing to begin. But Mari's compassion is something that I will never forget, and her sweet and giving nature surely remained in the hearts of all her beloved retired friends.

7.

Chapter Seven:

Sacred Girl as a Marigold—You Grow, Girl!

Marigold (flower): Full of joyful, strong, healing energy; longevity and protection.

The Girl in the Know

Oh, ladies, you know who I'm talking about. We all know her, though she goes by a different name in every town. She's a little plump—heck, let's tell it like it is. She's fat. Or no, wait…she's skinny! All planes and angles, with about as many curves as a butter knife. No matter what her shape is, she wears brightly colored t-shirts that lovingly caress it. She walks with a spring in her step, her head held high. She smiles openly, warmly, and fearlessly at everyone she meets, and she captivates all with her bright eyes and contagious laughter. You've heard people whisper about her looks. "Why does she wear lip gloss when her lips are so huge?" they ask. "And that awful nose! Why would anyone with that nose actually get a *nose ring*?" Although boys tell her that she should

a)   grow her hair long
b)   cut her hair short
c)   get it straightened
d)   get a perm
e)   dye it
f)   get extensions,

she just smiles and says, "You know, I think I'll wear it like this…until I decide I need a change." Then she turns away,

g)   swinging her wild curls
h)   swaying her straight locks
i)   patting her afro
j)   rubbing her bald head
k)   twisting on her dreadlock/braid/ponytail
l)   running her fingers through her spikes,

and goes about her business, wondering for the millionth time why others don't do the same.

Strangely enough, both guys and girls flock to her like moths to a flame. They are respectful, awestruck, humbled, and confused by her. What, for crying out loud, is her secret? The truth is, *she has ancient knowledge.* And what she knows is that she is a queen. She doesn't think it, she knows it, and not because she has a boyfriend or girlfriend that tells her that she's pretty, or because she has a dad that calls her "Princess." If you asked her, she probably couldn't pinpoint exactly how she came upon this knowledge, but she is astute enough to know that not every woman has it. And she thinks that's a shame.

I've heard ancient knowledge called different things throughout my life, the most popular label being "woman's intuition." I've also heard "voice within," "instinct," and others that haven't stuck with me because they sounded silly or condescending to my ears. Intuition, or whatever you want to call it, is the voice of your Higher Power whispering divine truths in your ear. People often ignore this voice or allow it to be drowned out by the noise and confusion of their busy lives.

Since time began, women have been wounded, but we have never been defeated. A woman can have one arm and one leg in casts, and still manage to earn money, clean her house, and feed her kids. That is the miracle, the mystery, and the magic of womanhood.

The Power of Joy: Your Feminine Spirit

I have good news, and I have bad news. Which do you want first? Oh, never mind all that...

The good news is, you are a glorious manifestation of all that is good. You are a queen, or a young princess on her way to queendom. You hold your head up high, and you love yourself enough to never have to put others down to gratify yourself. You are an adored child of God, by whichever name you call Him or Her. You respect your mother Earth, she respects you back, and it shows in the way you carry yourself with pride and grace.

The bad news is, it is likely that many of the people you know will not appreciate the fact that you believe in yourself, love yourself, and know that you are loved by your God. "Look at that haughty girl!" they think, "Who does she think she is?" You may do nothing more outrageous than smile when others insult you or walk away when someone is mean to you. Young girls must relearn to honor the feminine. Women are frequently condescended in our society and dishonored for expressing themselves with passion and depth. I cringe to admit it, but sometimes this happens in my own home! If I'm expressing myself with emotion or ferocity, my husband often asks, "Are you PMS-ing?" As if something is chemically wrong with me every time I'm emotional! This really burns me up. Sadly, many women have fallen into this self-loathing, self-denying pattern of thinking, thereby giving certain people exactly what they want. Denying our feminine spirit only impedes our ability to flourish. When the soul suckers fail to hit their mark, they become quite flustered and confused. But that's their problem. Your spirit is strong, safe, and whole. Because of that, some people will feel threatened by, and fearful of, your power. Too bad for them! Do not let the negative energy of others dilute the divine feminine force that is your birthright.

Part of that force involves celebrating our playful nature, the creative, giggly, silly self that fuels and inspires girls. The scared, insecure people that support our "masculine" culture continue to try to destroy the feminine spirit. One day, when I was working with teens, I got a call from my best friend, Erica. She had gone into labor! I was ecstatic at the news of my goddaughter's impending birth. Yeah, I know I have six godchildren, but my excitement was barely contained. I beamed with happiness for the rest of my shift, knowing that so far, the birthing process was going smoothly. As I walked towards the parking lot at the end of the day, some girls were outside breaking down cardboard boxes. I stopped to chat with them, telling them that I was on my way to the hospital to be with my friend. We laughed and talked happily for a few minutes. One girl said, "This box is so big, I bet I could fit my whole body inside!" I replied, "I'm bigger than you, and I bet even I could fit in there!" I stepped into the box, confirming that indeed, the box was big enough. We giggled for no apparent reason, and I waved goodbye as I left for the day.

The birth went beautifully, and my gorgeous godchild was born healthy. The next day, I was called into the office of Larry, one of my supervisors. He informed me that a male coworker had seen me playing with the girls and had reported that I was encouraging playfulness when the girls were supposed to be hard at work. I had, in fact, *behaved playfully* during a time that had not been specifically designated for play, and had done so for a full *five minutes*!!! My mouth agape with surprise, Larry went on to say that if he himself had caught me behaving in this manner, he would have "embarrassed" me by reprimanding me on the spot. I was stunned. But, just momentarily. Then I responded, "As you are probably aware, I am in a pretty good mood most of the time. I happened to be in a very good mood due to the coming of my new godbaby. I shared my mood with the girls. Feel free to publicly reprimand me for happiness any time you want to." Larry was somewhat taken aback by my lack of apology; nevertheless, I didn't hear from him ever again about my behavior. And I didn't change one bit, so I guess his threat didn't have the desired effect. The coworker who reported me became strangely uncomfortable when the girls were being "girly" (playful, passionate, and in charge at the same time) or when the female staff encouraged their fun, fiery natures.

As I've said before, it's a shame when people are threatened by the feminine spirit, but it is our gift from the Goddess, and it can't be subdued. If we constantly shrink like wilted flowers under the disapproval of others, the world of women will become a dying, droopy garden. This is my vow, my affirmation for every day:

I celebrate the feminine spirit in all her unbridled glory, and I will protect her from anyone who tries to shut her down.

Bring Her to Life:

Uncovering the Best Kept Secret in the West

Western culture is chock-full of messages that tell us that men are the superior sex, busy as bees doing manly things in a manly style. Have you ever seen the beer commercial where the boys are playing sports, having oodles of fun, getting all dirty and sweaty, and there's a pair of beautiful, half-naked twin girls standing on the sidelines? The girls, of course, don't talk, not even to each other. Perhaps they have nothing to say? Oh, I know! They don't know *how* to talk! All kidding aside, we all know, including the young girls who see this commercial, that the twins are there for one reason: eye candy for the boys, an eager, sexually available audience to their macho activity. Now don't get me wrong; I'm not a "player-hater" with a grudge against beautiful twins. On the contrary, I love it when women are confident in their looks, and not afraid to enjoy their own beauty. I'm also no stranger to the joys of watching cute guys play sports. What bothers me is the widespread media image of the brainless, mute hottie who's only ambition is to be…well, she has no ambition. Heck, she can't even spell ambition! This image is damaging to young women and girls and serves two purposes: to throw gas on the flames of low self-esteem, and to perpetuate the idea that men are the powerful ones, and that's the way it's going to stay— girls on the sidelines.

When Americans read "In God We Trust" on our currency, or recite "…one nation, under God, with liberty and justice for all," aren't most of us thinking of "God" in masculine terms? On the other hand, we generally understand God to be the Great Spirit, not a physical presence. Of course, Jesus was a man, as was Buddha, as is the pope, and most clergy in the U.S. All of the U.S. presidents have been men, most government officials, world leaders, and television network executives. So isn't it natural for us girls to "know our place" without having to be told?

The ancient belief in the feminine divine is rejected quite fearfully in our culture. Even in Catholicism, Mary (Jesus's own mother, for goodness' sake!) is to be revered, loved, respected, and prayed to, but not *worshipped*. The truth is, in cultures around the world, the feminine divine, the goddess, is alive and well, and has never been otherwise. Furthermore, the goddess's strength is not perceived as being a masculine quality. If, as is the Christian belief, we humans are created in

God's image, then doesn't that mean that God is both masculine and feminine? God and Goddess, two sides of the same divine coin, existing in harmony with one another? The masculine and feminine divine are not at war, fighting to gain dominance, with the goddess barely holding her ground amongst the natives in some far-off, primitive land. The Divine Spirit is too busy loving, protecting, and guiding us to bother with such trivialities. Women all over the world, even in the U.S., are coming back to the ancient ways, understanding that we represent the feminine face of the Divine. But our journey to this understanding is fraught with stumbling blocks, and we are the only ones who can stop them from impeding our progress. We have to ignore negative images of ourselves in the media. We have to join with other girls so we can encourage and support each other. We have to remember that our spirit is where we truly live, and it has to be strengthened and cared for just as much as our bodies. We have to start believing in, and celebrating, ourselves as little girls; and when we become women, we have to help other girls understand that they absolutely should know their places: not on the sidelines, but in the game.

Gunas: Moving Peacefully Down the Path

One thing that I have discovered in my work with girls is that the desire to follow their own spiritual paths makes them very enthusiastic at first. They feel called to connect to their Higher Power. The concept of the feminine divine feels familiar to them, like maybe they forgot something important. "That's right!" they exclaim, snapping their fingers. "I am a child of the Goddess! I am a queen!" They meditate with fervor, feng shui their living spaces, and begin to pray a lot. Keeping up the pace of speedy spirituality is tough, though, and it's not likely to create a lasting change if not taken thoughtfully and peacefully. I have said many times that the path is a process—a stroll through the garden, not a sprint to the finish line. In Sankhya, a type of Indian philosophy, this spiritual progression has three qualities known as *gunas*: *tamas* (ignorance, darkness, inertia), *rajas* (energy, passion, activity), and *sattva* (purity, light, goodness). If we are moving along the spiritual path properly, we go through the *gunas* from *tamas* to *sattva*, resisting the urge to get stuck somewhere in the first two, or getting burnt out during *rajas*.

Spiritual connection takes consistency and commitment. Like any relationship, your relationship with the spirit can't be neglected and expected to survive. Your Higher Power has been with you all along and will never leave you. It is *you* that has to open the door. Just like you brush your teeth every day (at least I hope you do), you have to make connecting with the spirit a daily habit. Even saying a brief prayer, blessing someone in need, or showing kindness with a smile or a helping hand, channels the spirit through you. Take matters into your own hands and be a conduit for fierceness, femininity, and love. As a woman, this is part of your birthright. Enjoy the journey...

Resources

Eating Disorders:

National Eating Disorders Association (NEDA)
phone: 1-800-931-2237
website: http://www.nationaleatingdisorders.org

Substance Abuse:

National Council on Alcoholism and Drug Abuse
phone: 1-800-622-2255
website: http://ncadd.org/

Partnership for a Drug-Free America
phone: 1-800-DRUGFREE
website: http://www.drugfree.org/

*Substance Abuse and Mental Health Services
Administration (SAMHSA)*
phone: 1-800-662-HELP (4357); for the hearing
impaired via TTY: 1-800-487-4889
website: http://www.samhsa.gov/

**If you need support due to a parent, caregiver, or
relative's substance abuse:

Al-Anon/Alateen
phone: 1-888-425-2666
wbsite: www.al-anon.alateen.org/

Mental Health, Suicide/Crisis:

Suicide Hotline
phone: 1-800-273-TALK
website: http://afsp.org/

The National Hopeline Network
phone: 1-800-784-2433 (1-800-SUICIDE)
website: https://hopeline.com/

The National Suicide Prevention Lifeline (24 hours a day, 7 days a week)
phone: 1-800-273-TALK (In Spanish: 1-888-628-9454; for the hearing impaired via TTY: 1-800-799-4889)
website: https://suicidepreventionlifeline.org/

The Trevor Project (LGBTQ youth)
phone: 1-866-488-7386
website: https://www.thetrevorproject.org/

Mental Health, Anxiety/Depression:

Anxiety Disorders Association of America (ADAA)
phone: 240-485-1001
website: www.adaa.org
email: information@adaa.org

Depression and Bipolar Support Alliance (DBSA)
phone: 800-826-3632
website:
        http://www.dbsalliance.org/site/PageServer?pagename=home

**Information for educators:
https://www.mentalhealth.gov/talk/educators/index.ht
ml

Abuse/Sexual Abuse/Rape/Incest:

Rape, Abuse, and Incest National Network
phone: 1-800-656-4673
website: http://www.rainn.org

National Domestic Violence Hotline
phone: 1-800-799-7233
website: http://www.ndvh.org

National Teen Dating Abuse Helpline
phone: 1-866-331-9474
website: http://www.loveisrespect.org

Bullying:

Speak Up: School Violence and Bullying
phone: 1-866-773-2587
website: http://www.cpyv.org

Cyberbullying:

website: http://stopbullying.gov/cyberbullying/

Bullying/LGBTQI:

website: http://stopbullying.gov/at-
risk/groups/lgbt/index.html

Cyber Tipline
phone: 1-800-843-5678
website: http://www.cybertipline.com

General Resources/Transgender Youth:

website:
      https://www.glaad.org/transgender/resources

Pregnancy/Birth Support:

American Pregnancy Helpline
phone: 1-866-942-6466
website: http://www.thehelpline.org

Planned Parenthood
phone: 1-800-230-7526
website: https://www.plannedparenthood.org/

Made in the USA
Las Vegas, NV
23 October 2025

32827972R00069